French New Wave

Chris Wiegand

www.pocketessentials.com

This edition published in July 2005 by Pocket Essentials
P.O.Box 394, Harpenden, Herts, AL5 1XJ
www.pocketessentials.com

Distributed in the USA by Trafalgar Square Publishing, P.O. Box 257, Howe Hill
Road, North Pomfret, Vermont 05053

A CIP catalogue record for this book is available from the British
Library.

ISBN 1 904048 44 7

2 4 6 8 10 9 7 5 3 1

Typeset by Avocet Typeset, Chilton, Aylesbury, Bucks
Printed and bound in Great Britain by Cox & Wyman, Reading

Acknowledgements

Thanks to Paul Duncan for providing unlimited editorial guidance and enthusiasm. Further assistance came from Shannon Attaway, Mylene Bradfield, Louise Cooper, Julia Dance, Lisa DeBell, Alexis Durrant, Lizzie Frith, Maria Kilcoyne, Steve Lewis, Wade Major, Ion Mills, Luke Morris, Gary Naseby, Matt Price, Jill Reading, Jessica Simon, James Spackman and Claire Watts. Merci à tous!

Contents

Making Waves: An Introduction   9

Birth of the Cool   31
Et Dieu Créa la Femme, Les Mistons, Ascenseur
Pour L'Echafaud, Le Beau Serge, Les Amants, Les
Cousins, Le Signe du Lion

Cannes '59   56
Les Quatre Cents Coups, Hiroshima Mon Amour

Guns, Girls and Gauloises   65
A Bout de Souffle, Tirez Sur le Pianiste

Les Femmes   75
Zazie Dans le Métro, Les Bonnes Femmes, Lola,
Jules et Jim

**And Godard Created Karina, then
Recreated Bardot**   89
Une Femme est Une Femme, Vivre sa Vie,
Le Mépris, Bande à Part

CONTENTS

Songs, Thrills and a Town Called Alphaville   **105**
La Peau Douce, Les Parapluies de Cherbourg, Alphaville, Pierrot le Fou

Further Viewing   **120**
A guide to other New Wave-related films

Reference Material   **152**
Recommended books and websites

Making Waves: An Introduction

Beautiful women. Suave leading men. Existential angst. Black and white figures in Parisian cafés. Cigarette smoke. Lots of it.

The world of French cinema conjures up a hundred often-parodied clichés for today's viewer and the films of the New Wave era supply their own set of distinctive images. Jean Seberg walking down the Champs Elysées selling the *New York Herald Tribune*. The young Jean-Pierre Léaud running through the streets of Paris with a stolen typewriter. Charles Aznavour playing honky-tonk piano in a run-down café. Anna Karina and Jean-Claude Brialy brushing off their feet before going to sleep. Eddie Constantine, decked out in gumshoe hat and mac, arriving at the sinister town of Alphaville. Jean-Paul Belmondo wrapping dynamite around his painted face. Brigitte Bardot lying naked in a bedroom asking Michel Piccoli what he thinks of her rear. Jeanne Moreau, Oskar Werner and Henri Serre cycling through the countryside. The list is endless.

These images are some of the things that the New Wave means to me, yet decades after the term was coined in *L'Express* magazine, critics continue to argue over its precise meaning. Some confine the New Wave to a certain period of time, others to particular directors.

Many believe that the film-makers who wrote for the influential journal *Cahiers du Cinéma* are the only ones we can truly describe as belonging to the New Wave. Among the directors believed at one time or another to be related to the movement are: Jean-Luc Godard, François Truffaut, Claude Chabrol, Jacques Rivette, Eric Rohmer, Alain Resnais, Louis Malle, Roger Vadim, Jacques Demy, Agnès Varda, Chris Marker, Jean Rouch, Jacques Rozier, Jean Douchet, Alexandre Astruc, Pierre Kast, Jacques Doniol-Valcroze and Jean Eustache.

Phew! This book doesn't set out to cover every film made by every film-maker connected with the movement. Space restrictions make such a task impossible. Instead, this guide looks at the early years of the movement named the Nouvelle Vague (New Wave). It examines the first works of some truly iconoclastic and innovative directors, and follows roughly a decade of film-making, from the mid-1950s to the mid-1960s. This was a time when the New Wave had a certain sense of cohesion, if not in real life then often thematically and stylistically on the screen.

In choosing the films to be covered, I have primarily given space to those works that made their directors' reputations during these years. As the temporal bias would have led to the exclusion of certain directors' key critical and commercial successes, such as Truffaut's *Le Dernier Métro*, Chabrol's *Le Boucher* and Rivette's *La Belle Noiseuse*, I have included a check list of other New Wave-related films at the end of the book. For these and the principal pictures discussed during the book, you'll find a short note about that film's availability on DVD or video.

Everyone's a Critic

Before examining their films, it is worth remembering that the principal New Wave directors started their cinematic careers as critics. Many continued to write criticism while filming their own works, seeing themselves as both critics and film-makers. This is not to say they were mere movie reviewers. They essentially redesigned the role of the film critic, recognising the medium as on a par with the other arts and giving detailed analysis to directors who had never before been treated with much respect. The birth of this new form of criticism – and of the New Wave itself – owes much to two men: Henri Langlois and André Bazin.

Across Paris at the end of the 1940s there was a large number of cinema clubs, where young intellectuals could view home-grown and foreign films, then discuss them to their heart's content with like-minded people. One of the best was Henri Langlois' Cinémathèque Française, which was co-founded with Georges Franju (who went on to direct *Les Yeux Sans Visage*) and opened its doors to cinéphiles in 1948. The Cinémathèque was a place for learning, not just watching. The cinema was a small one, consisting of just 50 seats, but Langlois had archived a wide range of films from around the world to screen to his eager audiences.

Many of the films shown in the cinema clubs at this time were American. During the Occupation, the import of Hollywood films to Europe had been banned by the Nazis so the French public had missed out on a period of particular fertility in US cinema. After the war, these missing films filtered through to France in rapid succession. This meant that, between 1946 and 1947, the young French critics were given a crash course in roughly ten years of American cinema, including masterpieces by the likes of John Ford and Alfred Hitchcock.

It was at the Cinémathèque Française that the principal movers in the New Wave originally met. One of the key figures, François Truffaut, already had an especially intense and involved relationship with the cinema. He had turned to films at an early age, finding them a kind of refuge from his unhappy home life with his mother and stepfather. Truffaut's teenage years were dogged by petty crime and a spell in a young offenders' institute. The cinema managed to give his life some sort of focus.

Jean-Luc Godard had a similarly passionate relationship with the movies. Godard was born in Paris but spent his childhood in Switzerland. Returning to his native France, he studied ethnology at the Sorbonne but, before long, found himself studying cinema in a far more intensive fashion at the Cinémathèque. His passion was also linked to a form of escapism. In his introduction to a volume of François Truffaut's letters, Godard described the cinema screen as 'the wall we had to scale in order to escape from our lives.' Rumours of the pair's early viewing sessions have reached mythic status. At one point, Godard alone was said to be watching around 1,000 films a year. But the life of the average cinéphile involved more than just viewing films. Stills and posters were collected, credits were studied for familiar names, and lists were compiled of favourites from different countries. Everything was done to put the work on screen into some kind of perspective.

Godard was intent on setting up a film journal that he could write for. He did so with Jacques Rivette, a young man from Rouen, and Eric Rohmer, a former literature teacher from Nancy. Rohmer was born Jean-Marie Maurice Scherer and chose his new name as a combination of director Erich von Stroheim and the novelist Sax Rohmer. Entitled *La Gazette du Cinéma*, this publication was to appear irregularly but, nevertheless, provided the critics with a suitable stamping ground to discuss the many films they were watching. Truffaut, Godard, Rohmer and Rivette, along with a young intellectual named Alain Resnais, were soon writing for a variety of magazines, including *Arts* and *Les Amis du Cinéma*.

The most important journal was *Cahiers du Cinéma* (formerly *La Revue du Cinéma*), which featured reviews and general discussions on cinema theory. The journal was founded in 1950 by André Bazin, Jacques Doniol-Valcroze and Lo Duca. The first issue hit the streets in April 1951. Rohmer, Godard and Rivette joined the journal in 1952. Rohmer went on to edit it from 1956 to 1963. At the time he joined, *Cahiers* was edited by Bazin, who had also run his own cinema club during the Occupation. At *Cahiers*, Bazin became something of a surrogate father to the young men and helped educate them in a manner similar to Langlois. He was to share a particularly close relationship with Truffaut who, after a brief meeting with the older man, had written to him from the young offenders' institute begging for help.

Favourite Film-Makers

The caustic *Cahiers* critics styled themselves as a 'band of outsiders', to quote the title of one of Jean-Luc Godard's later films. They were united by their disdain for the mainstream 'tradition de qualité,' which dominated the French film industry at the time. In a famous essay for *Cahiers* entitled 'Une certaine tendance du cinéma français,' published on New Year's Day in 1954, a 22-year-old Truffaut set out the New Wave's argument against the restrictive uniformity of the 'tradition de qualité.' Such film-making was confined to the studios and presented run-of-the-mill stories in an old-fashioned and unimaginative glossy style. These pictures were made with one eye firmly on the box office and they rarely challenged viewers. Singled out for criticism in Truffaut's article was the dominating role played by the scriptwriter. This outdated brand of cinema simply wasn't visual enough for the young critics, who quickly renamed it 'cinéma de papa' and took their inspiration from elsewhere.

They praised the French directors of an earlier era, such as the great social commentator Jean Renoir (*La Grande Illusion*) and the Poetic Realist Jean Vigo (*L'Atalante*), alongside contemporaries who had successfully made films outside the studio system, such as Jean-Pierre Melville (*Le Silence de la Mer*), who would become recognised as the godfather of the New Wave. The fact that Renoir and Melville not only directed, but also either wrote, produced or starred in many of their features, particularly inspired the *Cahiers* crowd. Other French film-makers admired by the critics included Henri-Georges Clouzot (*Le Corbeau*), Robert Bresson (*Mouchette*), René Clément (*Les Jeux Interdits*) and the collaborative works of Marcel Carné and Jacques Prévert (*Les Visiteurs du Soir*).

The critics looked outside France to find other directors who either refused to play the studio game or attempted to subvert it from within. Fritz Lang influenced them all. Godard would later cast Lang in his 1963 picture *Le Mépris*. Both Lang's early German work and his American movies inspired the New Wave critics. A number of distinctive American directors were extremely influential. The critics were never hierarchical when it came to praising film-makers and gave American B-movie directors such as Sam Fuller (*Shock Corridor*) and Jacques Tourneur (*Cat People*) a level of respect many found hard to understand at the time. These days, critical studies of Hitchcock dominate the film section of any bookshop, but Chabrol and Rohmer's decision to write a book on Hitch was considered extraordinary in the 1950s.

Another European influence on the New Wave was Italy's neorealism movement. Directors like Roberto Rossellini and Vittorio De Sica showed that it was possible to make dramatic and incredibly moving films outside the studio, working on location and using non-professionals who often improvised their lines. Neorealist directors removed the heavy noise insulation from cameras, using them in a hand-held fashion and shooting without sound, which they post-synchronised later. The neorealists showed the financial advantages of such a style of film-making, as well as the liberating creative advantages.

La Politique des Auteurs

This personal approach to film-making appealed to the New Wave critics, who were by now recognising the importance of the director as an auteur. That is to say, they believed that of all the people involved in the making of a film, the director is the only real author of the end product. This is a theory that is pretty much taken for granted these days, as people will speak of going to see "the new Woody Allen film" or "Spike Lee's latest," but in the 1950s it was considered a radical new approach to cinema. Previously, films had been viewed as the product of a particular studio or producer and less respect had been given to the director.

Of course, this theory was not true for every film produced. As exponents of the auteur theory, the New Wave critics singled out Americans such as Nicholas Ray, Orson Welles, Howard Hawks and John Ford, whose works they had enjoyed at the Cinémathèque. They demonstrated convincingly, in essays for *Cahiers,* that the films of such directors consistently bore the unique mark of an individual, just as the collected novels of a certain author were commonly accepted as bearing similarities in terms of style, theme and subject matter. In the auteur fashion, films were equated with other works of art and were not considered – as had been commonly accepted – the product of a mass commercial operation. To look at films as the product of a sole imagination and not a faceless studio beast required that the cinema be viewed as more personal and intimate than ever before.

The critic Alexandre Astruc had put forward the

notion of the 'caméra-stylo' or 'camera-pen' in an article in *L'Ecran Français,* in March 1948, and his manifesto had been quickly accepted by the *Cahiers* critics. In the essay, Astruc argued that the cinema could have its own 'language' just like the other arts. The *Cahiers* critics' writings meant that cinema's low-brow reputation and short history (it was just 60 years young at the time) was reassessed. Suddenly, certain westerns and gangster movies were equated in terms of artistic merit to impressionist paintings and classic novels.

First Film-Making Experiences

Not content with watching and writing about films, the *Cahiers* critics wanted to get to grips with the film industry from a variety of angles. Chabrol worked for a period as a publicist at 20th Century Fox, where he was also able to secure a job for Godard as a press agent. Godard also worked for the Swiss national TV network, while Truffaut gained some experience in the film unit of the Ministry of Agriculture. Some were lucky enough to learn their craft alongside their cinematic idols. Truffaut cut his teeth with Max Ophüls and Roberto Rossellini. Jacques Rivette worked with Jean Renoir and his disciple Jacques Becker (*Touchez Pas au Grisbi*). Louis Malle collaborated with the explorer Jacques-Yves Cousteau and with Jacques Tati and Robert Bresson.

By the early 1950s the *Cahiers* critics had started to make their first short films. Rohmer directed *Journal D'un Scélérat* while Chabrol wrote the screenplay for Rivette's first short, *Le Coup du Berger.* Financial backing was sometimes hard to find for these first cinematic ventures and each of the young directors had to devise new ways to gain funding. Godard was perhaps the most successful among them. In 1952 he wrote, produced, directed and edited the 20-minute documentary *Opération Béton*, which concerned the building of the Grande Dixene dam in the Dix Valley, Switzerland. He made the film with the wages he had earned working as a labourer on the dam and, once it was completed, he sold the documentary to the company who had undertaken the work on the dam, thus providing the funds for his own first dramatic shorts.

A New Formula

When the *Cahiers* critics came to make feature films themselves, they knew that they would be made firmly in the auteur's mould. But how would the opportunity come about? Film-making had always been an expensive business. It was extremely hard to make a film without the financial backing of a major studio. The equipment involved was costly and hard to come by. The explosion of the New Wave onto cinema screens across France and around the world came down partly to coincidence. As it happens, the critics were forming such notions of independent film-making at a time of great technological and social change, which would help them to put their notions into practice. As the money-grabbing movie producer Battista comments, in Alberto Moravia's novel *Il Disprezzo* (filmed by Godard as *Le Mépris*), 'The after-the-war period is now over, and people are feeling the need of a new formula.'

After the war, the Gaullist government brought in film subsidies for new productions and film-making equipment itself also became cheaper, due partly to the rise of television. Developments in documentary film-making meant that lighter and cheaper hand-held cameras, such as the Eclair, Cameflex and Arriflex had become more widely available and affordable to young directors. Faster film stock that could be used in darker conditions (thus outside the studio) had also been successfully developed. Synchronous sound recorders and lighting equipment became equally affordable and portable. These breakthroughs meant directors no longer needed a studio to make a film, as real locations provided free, authentic backdrops. Crews became smaller and in general the critics were able to make their first films very cheaply. Suddenly, film-makers had more choice over the kind of film that they wanted to make and who would appear in it.

The odds for the finished product were also changing. Before this time, anyone venturing to make their own film outside of help from the studios would see that film given an extremely limited release, mainly in the obscure arthouse cinemas. Because of the US government's anti-trust legislation, which effectively ended the studios' domination, smaller films success-fully received more widespread distribution. For the first time, they were screened at mainstream cinemas as well as arthouse venues. The New Wave reached the cinemas and audiences were unable to ignore it.

A Portrait of Today's Youth

This collection of circumstances signalled record numbers of first-time film-makers in France. Over 20 directors released their first films in 1959 and this number doubled in the following year. These figures were extraordinary for the time. In the 1950s most directors made their debut at around the age of 40, after serving a lengthy apprenticeship. Remarkably, not only were these youngsters making their own films, many were doing extremely well at the box office.

Film-making was suddenly a fresh and youthful force, as new pictures were made by, for and starring young people. In the 1950s, this coincided with the American youth culture explosion created by rock and roll. When Roger Vadim's *Et Dieu Créa la Femme* was released in America in 1957 it was heralded as a female, French counterpart to the quintessential American youth movie *Rebel Without a Cause*. Many New Wave films spoke to young audiences about their lives. They were shot in the present day and applicable to modern issues, unlike the outdated costume dramas churned out by the 'cinéma de papa.'

The playfulness, rebelliousness and inventiveness of the first New Wave films reveal the tender age of their directors. It is telling that the term 'Nouvelle Vague' was coined in a 1957 article in *L'Express* that was entitled 'Report On Today's Youth.' The article, written by the journalist Françoise Giroud, dealt primarily with society, as did the book she published the following year, *The New Wave: Portrait of Today's Youth*. The phrase 'new wave' was bandied about to represent a whole generation as well as a film-making movement. However, the term stuck to the cinematic works that kicked up a storm two years later at the Cannes Film Festival.

New Wave Style

So how can we define a New Wave film? A clue is offered by a character in Godard's 1962 picture *Vivre sa Vie*, who comments of her reading material, "The story's dumb but it's very well written." For most of the New Wave directors (and Godard in particular) the manner in which the movie's story was told became far more important than ever before. It usually became more important than the story itself. "Because they reject complicated plots, the films may look like shorts stretched out to feature length," observed François Truffaut of the "so-called New Wave film" in *Sight and Sound* (Winter Issue, 1961). The *Cahiers* directors broke with traditional narrative conventions, favouring arresting and stylish techniques such as the jump-cut (a cut that literally jumps from one point in time to another). Shot off the cuff on real locations, often with a cast encouraged to improvise, their pictures have a spontaneous and unpredictable nature. The directors displayed a pick 'n' mix approach to filmmaking, audaciously whisking together their films' modern elements with classic silent techniques such as intertitles (often used by Godard) and irises (favoured by Demy).

The Men who Loved Films

New Wave films are also marked by an unconditional love for the cinema that often manifested itself in a series of playful ways. Truffaut asked himself the question, 'Is cinema more important than life?' and the answer for him and the other *Cahiers* critics was, more often than not, in the affirmative. New Wave directors were never afraid to remind their audiences they were watching a film. Characters spoke directly to the camera and films would often open with extreme close-ups. The pictures of the *Cahiers* critics became films about films, full of the sorts of in-jokes and cinematic references that you would expect from a school of critics/film-makers who scoured their favourite films like magpies. Influential directors such as Jean-Pierre Melville and Sam Fuller were cast in cameo roles. Key scenes paid tribute to earlier works by respected auteurs and posters of well-respected films crept their way into the background. Godard and Truffaut both went on to make movies that were expressly about the process of making a film.

As an indication of the extent of cinematic references in the films, it is extraordinary to see just how many characters in New Wave films go to the cinema themselves. The films are littered with trips to the movies. In *Vivre sa Vie*, Nana weeps during a screening of *La Passion de Jeanne D'Arc*. In *Les Quatre Cents Coups*, Antoine and René bunk off school to go to the cinema. In *Jules et Jim*, the lead characters are reunited by a chance meeting in a cinema. Michel and Patricia hide from the authorities in a picture house in *A Bout de Souffle*. If the characters weren't watching movies they might be talking about them or reading about them – spot the copies of *Arts* and *Cahiers* in Godard's *Charlotte et Véronique, ou Tous les Garçons S'Apellent Patrick.*

The Men who Loved Books

As the auteur theory and the notion of the 'camera-pen' suggest, the New Wave was an overwhelmingly literary movement. The New Wave directors were, like all film-makers and like many of the characters in their own movies, primarily interested in telling stories. The principal directors of the movement were critics, to whom expression through words was as important as expression on screen. Eric Rohmer had also worked on newspapers and published a novel under a pseudonym before he became interested in films. Alain Resnais was a literature teacher. Claude Chabrol had detective stories published before he became a director.

The New Wave directors spoke of their work in literary terms, especially Agnès Varda, who called it 'cinécriture.' Many were influenced by authors as well as film-makers. Balzac was a favourite writer with Truffaut in particular. In his debut feature, *Les Quatre Cents Coups*, Truffaut's young hero Antoine Doinel would create a shrine to the great writer. Truffaut's first real love was for books – a passion he had picked up from his grandmother. The director claimed that if he hadn't become a director he would have been a publisher.

New Wave scripts were often written by the directors themselves, but a startling number were adaptations of novels, ranging from pulp American thrillers to French romances. The diversity of the directors' source material can be seen in a list of the authors whose work they adapted: David Goodis, Alberto Moravia, Henri-Pierre Roché, Cornell Woolrich, Henry Miller, Lionel White, Ray Bradbury, Georges Simenon, Richard Stark, Gustave Flaubert, Ed McBain, Raymond Queneau and Simone de Beauvoir. This number of adaptations may seem surprising, considering the *Cahiers* critics' disapproval of the 'tradition de qualité.' However, what annoyed the critics were these film-makers' 'safe' adaptations of tame work, in which the film-making process brought little itself to the original material.

La Politique des Copains

The main players in the New Wave had a firm policy of helping each other to establish themselves – a commitment that's been labelled a 'politique des copains.' It is perhaps this collaborative policy that created the stylistic similarities between the films of the New Wave. In the early days, the same members of cast and crew were used by more than one director. Agnès Varda's low-budget short *La Pointe Courte* was edited by Alain Resnais who also cut Truffaut's first short, *Une Visite*, upon which Rivette worked as cameraman. Rivette's *Le Coup du Berger* featured cameos from Truffaut and Godard. Godard's *Charlotte et Véronique, ou Tous les Garçons S'Apellent Patrick* was based on a screenplay written by Rohmer. (An irreverent lesson in the art of seduction, this is one of the few early New Wave shorts easily available on DVD. It's included among works from Patrice Leconte, Nanni Moretti and others on the *Cinema16: European Short Films* DVD.)

Sometimes the directors swapped projects for one reason or another. Truffaut passed on to Godard 400 feet of film he had shot observing the floods in Paris, and from these beginnings, Godard made *Une Histoire d'Eau* (1958), acting as screenwriter, director and editor. The result was a pacy and often surprisingly lyrical short film where aerial, documentary-style footage of the floods is combined with a loose narrative. Godard's feature debut, *A Bout de Souffle*, would similarly be sparked by a treatment from Truffaut.

As they made a name for themselves, the New Wave directors continued to use the same team members in subsequent projects. This is especially true of Godard, who collaborated with the producer Georges de Beauregard throughout the 1960s. Truffaut used executive producer Marcel Berbet on 15 of his films and also regularly used the same editors: Claudine Bouché, Agnès Guillemot, Martine Barraqué and Yann Dedet. Chabrol continually favoured crew members such as photographer Jean Rabier and editors Jacques Gaillard and Monique Fardoulis. The same cinematographers, notably former Air Force cameraman Henri Decaë and one-time photographer and reporter Raoul Coutard, were used by most of the directors. Chabrol usually favoured Decaë, while Godard worked mostly with Coutard. Resnais often worked with Sacha Vierny, and Rohmer with Nicholas Hayer. Nestor Almendros photographed films for both Truffaut and Rohmer.

Screenwriting too, was often a collaborative affair. Claude Chabrol's scripts were often written with his friend Paul Gégauff, who also wrote screenplays for Eric Rohmer and Barbet Schroeder. Another screen-writer, Jean Gruault, wrote for Truffaut and Resnais and also made appearances in films directed by Godard and Truffaut. The two key figures behind the soundtracks for New Wave films are Michel Legrand and Georges Delerue. Legrand is best known for his scores for Jacques Demy's films, particularly *Les Parapluies de Cherbourg*, but he also worked extensively with Godard, as well as with Demy's wife, Agnès Varda. Delerue meanwhile provided the moving score for Godard's *Le Mépris* and worked with Truffaut, Malle, Varda and Resnais. The veteran Paul Misraki was recruited by Godard, Becker, Vadim and Chabrol.

Chabrol regularly re-cast specific actors such as Jean-Claude Brialy and Michel Bouquet in his films, while Godard frequently worked with Jean-Paul Belmondo. Truffaut cast Jean-Pierre Léaud as his alter ego in the Antoine Doinel films. Both Chabrol and Godard frequently cast their wives in lead roles. Stéphane Audran appears in some 20 films directed by Chabrol, while Karina stars in most of Godard's key 1960s features. The critic Michel Marie has compared Godard and Karina's partnership to that of Marlene Dietrich and Josef von Sternberg. Other actresses, such as Bernadette Lafont and Jeanne Moreau soon became inseparable from the movement.

Influence of the French New Wave

In their depiction of everyday contemporary life, the work of many French New Wave directors parallels the films of the British critic-directors associated with the Free Cinema documentary movement, such as Tony Richardson, Karel Reisz and Lindsay Anderson. The films of these British directors also told simple stories in a new and inventive style. They were often based on plays and the settings were usually domestic interiors, which led to them being labelled as 'kitchen sink' dramas. The plots of pictures such as Richardson's *A Taste of Honey* revolved around youthful lovers from working-class backgrounds, while solitary figures were presented as the 'angry young man' in films like *Look Back in Anger* and *The Loneliness of the Long Distance Runner*.

The French New Wave has had an immeasurable influence on American film-making. The first works of the *Cahiers* critics appeared at the same time as those of the American king of independent film-making, John Cassavetes, a director who also relied on financial assistance from friends to see his projects through to the big screen. With its jazzy score, natural performances, hand-held camerawork and liberal use of locations, Cassavetes' innovative debut *Shadows* bears remarkable similarities to *A Bout de Souffle*. Godard dedicated two of his films to the American actor-director, whose working relationship with wife Gena Rowlands (the star of *A Woman Under the Influence*) could easily be compared to that of Godard and Anna Karina's.

The New Wave directors' influence on their own national cinema was such that a later generation of French film-makers were labelled (imaginatively enough) the New New Wave. This new generation displayed a similar tendency to quote from the work of their cinematic heroes. Best of the bunch was Jean-Jacques Beineix, who arrived on the scene with the cult success *Diva* in 1980 and, like François Truffaut, went on to make a David Goodis adaptation for his second film (*La Lune dans le Caniveau*). Beineix is best known for *Betty Blue*, a visually arresting tale of *amour fou* starring Béatrice Dalle.

Two other stars of the New New Wave were Luc Besson and Leos Carax. Besson found early international success in 1985 with *Subway*, a thriller that took place in the Paris underground tunnels. His breathtaking diving drama *Le Grand Bleu* (*The Big Blue*) proved to be the most successful film in the 1980s in France and he sealed his reputation in the 1990s with two urban thrillers: *Nikita* and *Léon*. Leos Carax, from a later generation of *Cahiers du Cinéma* critics, won acclaim for his films *Mauvais Sang* and *Les Amants du Pont Neuf.* The directors of the New New Wave, whose style of film-making became known as the 'cinéma du look,' were sometimes dismissed as flashy and insubstantial.

The New Wave has also echoed through to the recent digital revolution and the Dogme95 manifesto, reverberating in the work of a new generation of independents from Scandinavia, such as Lars Von Trier and Kristian Levring. Just as technological advances in the 1950s changed the way that young directors made films, so developments in digital video have influenced the work of today's new film-makers.

Stylistically, the modern American director most often linked to the New Wave is Quentin Tarantino, who named his own production company A Band

Apart after Godard's *Bande à Part* and used part of the film as the basis for the dance scene in *Pulp Fiction*. Tarantino also named the diamond store in *Reservoir Dogs* 'Karina's'. Like Steven Soderbergh (*Out of Sight*), Tarantino shares the New Wave's love for unconventional narrative structure, as well as its tendency towards cinematic self-consciousness and in-jokes. The characters in Tarantino's films spend almost as much time watching movies as those in Godard and Truffaut's. The generic playfulness of Tarantino's first films recalls Godard's early work and *Tirez Sur le Pianiste*.

The New Wave in the New Century

New Wave nostalgia has been rekindled in recent years by two new movies. Written by Gilbert Adair and directed by Bernardo Bertolucci, *The Dreamers* painted a love triangle against the canvas of the événements in Paris in 1968. The central characters are all regulars at the Cinémathèque who divide their time between watching films and talking about them. *The Dreamers* bustles with in-jokes and references, quoting *A Bout de Souffle* as well as classic American films like *Top Hat* and *Scarface*. Paying homage to the New Wave with rather more turbulent results was Jonathan Demme's ill-conceived *Charade* remake *The Truth about Charlie*, worth watching only for the very welcome presence of Anna Karina and Charles Aznavour.

Meanwhile, the emergence of classic New Wave titles on DVD keeps the movement in the press, on screens and in the public's consciousness. In 2001 a complete Godard retrospective was held at London's

National Film Theatre, boasting a new print of *Bande à Part*. Since then, the NFT has afforded retrospectives to both Eric Rohmer and Jean-Pierre Melville. At the time of writing, the BFI is preparing to release new prints of Rivette's *Paris Nous Appartient* and *Céline et Julie Vont en Bateau*.

Truffaut, Malle and Demy may be gone but several of the movement's key directors remain bracingly prolific. Chabrol turned in his 50th film in 1997 and is still going strong although his latest, *La Demoiselle d'Honneur*, met with mixed reviews. In 2001 Godard, Rivette and Rohmer unveiled new movies (*Eloge de L'Amour*, *Va Savoir* and *L'Anglaise et le Duc* respectively), receiving high-profile attention in the international press. All three saw the directors in their finest form for years and were later matched by another raft of impressive titles: *Notre Musique*, *Histoire de Marie et Julien* and *Triple Agent*. Such typically probing, provocative works show that the directors of the Nouvelle Vague are still far from becoming French cinema's old guard.

Birth of the Cool

In many ways the story of the French New Wave begins in the summer of 1956 at Saint Tropez, where a 28-year-old writer-director named Roger Vadim made his first film. *Et Dieu Créa la Femme* was ostensibly a love letter to the beauty of his wife, former model and dancer Brigitte Bardot, who was only 22 at the time. Vadim's debut celebrated youth and vitality on screen and proved that small, low-budget films made by first-timers could do big box office both at home and abroad. The film met with hysteria in America and fared so well outside France that it was granted a re-release in its own country a year after it was first screened. It inspired a new generation of directors (Truffaut praised it in a review for *Cahiers*) and introduced the public to the charms of the lady who became known purely as BB.

Et Dieu Créa la Femme (1956)

Alternative Titles: *And God Created Woman, And Woman... Was Created*

Cast: Brigitte Bardot (Juliete Hardy), Curt Jürgens (Eric Carradine), Jean-Louis Trintignant (Michel

Tardieu), Jane Marken (Madame Morin), Jean Tissier (M Vigier-Lefranc), Isabelle Corey (Lucienne).

Crew: Directed by Roger Vadim. Written by Roger Vadim and Raoul Lévy. Produced by Claude Ganz and Raoul Lévy. Cinematography by Armand Thirard. Music by Paul Misraki. 91 mins.

Story: Juliete Hardy, a coquettish 18-year-old orphan, whiles away her time in Saint Tropez by avoiding employment and working instead at being happy. Living with her elderly and disapproving foster mother, Juliete can be found behind the till of the corner shop or sunning herself in a series of scantily clad poses that attract interest from the town's male community. She becomes enamoured first with local lad Antoine then with both his younger brother Michel and successful, scheming businessman Eric.

Background: With its sultry jazz score and liberal use of locations, *Et Dieu Créa la Femme* pre-empted the sound and look of many New Wave features. Representing irrepressible spirit and rebellious youth, Bardot revels in the role of Juliete and nabs the best lines in a fizzy script. Her sex kitten pose was to be much imitated in the following years, all too often by Bardot herself. Juliete is a rather more rounded character than is usually remembered. She is both wild cat and orphan victim, misunderstood by society and isolated from her family. In this fashion she foreshadows the restless, rootless male protagonists of *Les Quatre Cents Coups* and *A Bout de Souffle*. Freely admitting she wouldn't make a good wife because she likes fun too much, the passionate and audacious Juliete lives – in the manner of Belmondo's Michel Poiccard – as if she is going to die tomorrow. Her spontaneous nature is aided by the fact that Bardot was encouraged to bring her own traits to the part.

The quintessential 'new woman' of the New Wave, Juliete's quest for sexual fulfilment and her stubborn determination to live life by her own set of rules, was later taken up on screen by Jeanne Moreau. Her independence and free will are also echoed in the character of Patricia Franchini in *A Bout de Souffle*. Both Juliete and Patricia are relaxed with their sexuality and freely admit to having slept with numerous partners, representing the new morals of the teenager. Patricia smirks and holds up seven fingers when she is asked how many men she slept with in New York, while Juliete makes her way through a number of conquests in the film's 91 minutes.

The title of Vadim's film still conjures up a sense of the erotic. Considered sensationally promiscuous on its initial release, it is of course extremely tame by today's standards. You might try watching it in a double bill with writer-director Catherine Breillat's French sexathon *Romance*. From the very opening sequence onwards, the camera lingers amorously over Bardot's body, much as it will in the prologue of Godard's *Le Mépris*, the film that proved Bardot could act as well as pout.

In-Jokes: Setting the tone for the New Wave films that followed, both Vadim and co-screenwriter Lévy make brief cameo appearances.

The Verdict: 'But the devil invented Brigitte Bardot!' The tagline still says it all: BB lights up the screen, especially in the closing scene where she dances to the bongos in an underground club. However, she's unable to save Vadim's first film from its clunking longueurs and melodramatic excess. Heaps better than the director's 1987 picture of the same name though. 2/5

Availability: VHS (Arrow) and Region 2 DVD (C'est La Vie) with photo gallery, trailer reel and filmographies.

Now Try These: Vadim directed Bardot again in 1958's *Les Bijoutiers du Clair de Lune*, by which time they were divorced. Their fifth and final collaboration was the risqué and risible *Don Juan, ou Si Don Juan Etait Une Femme* (1973) with Jane Birkin.

At the end of summer 1957, Truffaut began shooting his bustling, freewheeling short *Les Mistons*, an adaptation of a story from Maurice Pons' *Les Virginales* collection. The shoot, which took place on location in Nîmes in the south of France, was facilitated by Truffaut's marriage to Madeleine Morgenstern, the daughter of a wealthy director of a number of film companies. Truffaut succeeded in forming his own production company, Les Films du Carrosse, in order to make the short. He thereby ensured both his independence and creative freedom on *Les Mistons* and future film projects. The company, which Truffaut was to run throughout his career, was named after Jean Renoir's 1953 film *Le Carrosse d'Or* starring Anna Magnani.

Les Mistons (1957)

Alternative Titles: *The Mischief Makers, The Brats*

Cast: Michel François (Narrator), Bernadette Lafont (Bernadette), Gérard Blain (Gérard).

Crew: Directed and written by François Truffaut. Based on a short story from *Les Virginales* by Maurice Pons. Produced by Robert Lachenay. Cinematography by Jean Malige. Music by Maurice Leroux. 17 mins.

Story: A barefooted young woman wearing a billowing skirt cycles towards the screen and rides into the countryside, where she is viewed by a group of enamoured boys. These are 'les mistons' – the lovesick youths who follow her every movement. Too young to court her, they spend their days trying to ruin her relationship with her boyfriend. When they hear of the girl's engagement they are horrified, but hope presents itself when her fiancé is drawn away from the village for military service.

Background: Truffaut once commented that he preferred to film women and children and in this respect, the nostalgic *Les Mistons* foreshadows his full-length features. Notable for its use of locations, *Les Mistons* is a breath of fresh air that also draws spontaneous, natural performances from its young stars and introduces two of the New Wave's most appealing faces: Bernadette Lafont and Gérard Blain. Truffaut's treatment is at times rough and ready, at others gracefully fluid, complementing Maurice Leroux's lilting music. Some of the gags, such as the old man with the garden hose, owe a debt to silent comedy. The scene in which the brats gun each other down with make-believe pistols pre-empts a similar shoot out in Godard's *Bande à Part*.

Half of Truffaut's films would be distilled from literary sources. This first adaptation contains whole chunks of Pons' original story, but one of the many ways in which Truffaut differed from the directors of the 'tradition de qualité' is that on the whole he didn't film straight literary adaptations, but rather used the source material as a basis for his own story. In *Tirez Sur le Pianiste*, his genre-crossing adaptation of David Goodis' crime novel *Down There*, Truffaut used the novel's plot as scaffolding for his film and considerably changed the tone of Goodis' original material.

In-Jokes: A real-life couple at the time, Lafont and Blain play characters sharing their own first names. At the cinema they watch *Le Coup du Berger*, a film made by *Cahiers* critic Jacques Rivette. A poster for *Chien Perdu Sans Collier* is torn off a wall by the boys.

The Verdict: Already, Truffaut reveals a masterly control of tone. *Les Mistons* has the tenderness of a first kiss and the cheekiness of a rudely blown raspberry. 3/5

Availability: Included on *Les Quatre Cents Coups* Region 2 DVD (Tartan). Also on *Les Quatre Cents Coups* VHS (Artificial Eye), deleted.

Now Try This: Truffaut's third film, *Jules et Jim*, is also set in the past and narrated by a wistful older man.

Louis Malle got his first experience working with the oceanographer Jacques-Yves Cousteau on the Palme d'Or-winning underwater documentary *Le Monde du Silence*. After this early success, Malle set about working on his first feature, an adaptation of a crime novel by Noël Calef. An ingenious, deliciously Hitchcockian thriller, *Ascenseur Pour L'Echafaud* was made in 1957 when its director was just 25 years old. In a December 1975 interview with *Films and Filming*, Malle was to remember: "We changed practically the whole story, just keeping the basic plot – the idea of a man trapped in an elevator for forty-eight hours over a weekend."

Despite having displayed considerable technical know-how on the documentary, Malle was an inexperienced movie director. In the lead female role, he cast Jeanne Moreau, who had started acting in her late teens and had become a familiar face of the Comédie Française. However, despite her theatrical success she had made do with bit parts on the big screen, over a period of ten years, until her appearance in *Ascenseur Pour L'Echafaud*. The presence of the older actress on set would prove reassuring for the relatively unseasoned Malle throughout the shoot.

Ascenseur Pour L'Echafaud (1958)

Alternative Titles: *Lift to the Scaffold, Frantic, Elevator to the Gallows*

Cast: Jeanne Moreau (Florence Carala), Maurice Ronet (Julien Tavernier), Georges Poujoly (Louis), Yori Bertin (Véronique), Jean Wall (Simon Carala).

Crew: Directed by Louis Malle. Written by Louis Malle and Roger Nimier. Based on the novel *Ascenseur Pour L'Echafaud* by Noël Calef. Produced by Jean Thuillier. Cinematography by Henri Decaë. Music by Miles Davis. 90 mins.

Story: Julien Tavernier, a young Parisian businessman and ex-Army officer, conspires with his lover, Florence, to murder her husband (and his boss), who is an important arms dealer. After much meticulous planning, Julien seems to commit the perfect murder, leaving Florence's husband dead in his office with his own gun in his hand. However, as he is about to drive away to meet Florence at a nearby café, he notices a piece of tell-tale evidence. Returning to the office, he becomes trapped in the lift. While he is stuck between floors, a local florist and her delinquent boyfriend, Louis, steal his car and drive past the café where Florence is waiting.

Florence sees the florist leaning out of the car's window, leading her to believe that Julien has backed out of the plan and taken off with a younger woman. Meanwhile, Louis and his girlfriend end up in the company of a couple of German tourists. That night the young couple try to steal the Germans' car. When they are interrupted, Louis shoots the tourists dead. This double murder leads to Julien (whose personal belongings are found at the scene of the crime) being hunted by the police.

Background: The first minutes of Malle's first fictional feature film are executed with impressive flair – watch the way the director cuts from the imminent assassination of Carala to the deafening whir of his secretary's electric pencil sharpener. *Ascenseur Pour L'Echafaud* emerges as an emotionally mature and classy thriller, its polished craftsmanship all the more impressive for being Malle's directorial debut. Although parts of the movie were shot in the studio, actual locations like the Champs Elysées were used effectively, notably in the scenes of Moreau searching for her lover through the streets of Paris.

For these tracking shots the camera was pushed along the road in a pram, pre-empting the guerrilla film-making tactics of Jean-Luc Godard and cinematographer Raoul Coutard in *A Bout de Souffle*. It's interesting to note quite how many New Wave films find their protagonists roaming aimlessly and desperately around the city like Florence. As a point of comparison, see Antoine Doinel's night in a printing factory in *Les Quatre Cents Coups* and Pierre's deserted days in *Le Signe du Lion*.

With its extreme opening close-ups, young cast and jazzy score, *Ascenseur Pour L'Echafaud* may easily be compared to Godard's feature debut *A Bout de Souffle*. However, the New Wave director who is most brought to mind during Malle's movie is François Truffaut, who put Moreau's breathy, impassioned voice-over to similarly good use in *Jules et Jim*. Godard, Truffaut and Malle all shared an interest in Hitchcock and in the thriller genre, especially the B-movie, and all three filmed adaptations of pulpy novels during their careers. Malle also whisked together different genres in the same manner as his contemporaries.

There's enough material packed into *Ascenseur Pour L'Echafaud* to fill three or four feature films. Malle veers between the different stories with ease, juggling Julien, Florence and the teenagers' fates, intermittently leaving each in a precarious cliff-hanger situation. He draws fine performances across the board, from Ronet and Moreau (both of whom he would work with again) to the younger actors. Like Truffaut, Malle would display a knack for extracting engaging turns from young stars.

This was also only the third film to be shot by Henri Decaë, one of the key cinematographers of the New Wave. As well as shooting on the streets of Paris in the evening, gloomy interiors were chosen such as the police interrogation room, the photographers' dark room and the lift itself, lit by the flame from Julien's cigarette lighter. Julien's gleaming knife, in these scenes, is just one of numerous shimmering surfaces in the film. The picture also makes imaginative use of other assorted light sources, including the night watchman's torch and car headlights.

In-Jokes: The German woman suggests that Véronique use her mini-camera to take photographs under the water. Could this be a tongue-in-cheek reference to Malle and Cousteau's *Le Monde du Silence*?

The Verdict: This unusual tale of a long journey to the end of the night was awarded the Prix Louis Delluc in France and has stood the test of time well. The magnificently knotty, potty plot delivers some real surprises and Miles Davis' sultry jazz soundtrack (recorded in one mammoth night-time session) deserves its awesome reputation. 3/5

Availability: VHS (Electric Pictures), deleted.

Now Try These: In 1958 Moreau also starred in another adaptation of a Calef novel, *Echec au Porteur*, directed by Gilles Grangier. Malle's 1971 coming-of-age drama *Le Souffle au Coeur* features original music from another jazz legend, Charlie Parker.

François Truffaut's acquaintance, Claude Chabrol, enjoyed the performances in *Les Mistons* so much that he cast Gérard Blain and Bernadette Lafont in his own first film, *Le Beau Serge*. The lead role was taken by Jean-Claude Brialy, who can be spotted playing chess in a brief scene in *Ascenseur Pour L'Echafaud*. Never one to do things by halves, Chabrol wrote, directed and produced the picture himself. Unlike most of the other New Wave directors, who had assisted their idols and dabbled with shorts before breaking through to features, he made *Le Beau Serge* without having had any previous experience of film-making. His debut picked up the Best Director prize at Locarno and was also awarded the Prix Jean Vigo.

Le Beau Serge (1958)

Alternative Titles: *Handsome Serge, Bitter Reunion*

Cast: Gérard Blain (Serge), Jean-Claude Brialy (François), Bernadette Lafont (Marie), Edmond Beauchamp (Glomaud), Michèle Méritz (Yvonne), Claude Cerval (Priest), André Dino (Michel), Jeanne Pérez (Madame Chaunier).

Crew: Directed, written and produced by Claude Chabrol. Cinematography by Henri Decaë and Jean Rabier. Music by Emile Delpierre. 95 mins.

Story: François, a young theology student, returns to the village of his youth after a period of 12 years. He is under doctor's orders to rest for the winter in order to recover from tuberculosis. Alighting from the bus and gathering his belongings, François is surprised to catch sight of a childhood friend, Serge, whom he hardly recognises. Rattled by Serge's unkempt appearance, François enquires after him at the village's guest house. He quickly gains a picture of his old friend's disillusionment.

Formerly a gifted student and promising architect, Serge now drinks all day and is trapped in a listless marriage with a girl who gave birth to a Down's syndrome child that died. She is now pregnant again and Serge believes the second baby will be similarly afflicted. François spends the evening at the guest house but the following morning he resolves to visit his old friend and rekindle their friendship.

Background: There is a strong sense of pride to *Le Beau Serge*'s opening statement, that the film was 'shot entirely in the parish of Sardent.' Chabrol himself had grown up in the village and his return home from the metropolis, to shoot the picture, offers a striking parallel to François' journey. Like *Les Mistons*, the film was made entirely on location, using natural light. It was mainly funded by the inheritance Chabrol received from his first wife. *Le Beau Serge* is often, and perhaps rather misleadingly, described as the first New Wave film. It's worlds apart from the debuts of Godard and Truffaut. While their first features concentrated on the joy and pain of urban dwelling, *Le Beau Serge* is a detailed record of working-class life in a bleak and wintry provincial village. Because of this proletariat perspective, Chabrol's film is more in the vein of directors like Renoir and Carné. As he would with his later works, Chabrol selected some memorable settings for the drama, from Serge's threadbare residence to a priest's chambers. The locations also occasionally mirror the plot, for François' old family home has gone to wreck and ruin much like Serge himself.

The dichotomy between Serge and François is set up perfectly in Chabrol's film. Serge often displays the traits of an immature child while François comes across as old before his time. Chabrol also draws a dramatic contrast between Blain and Brialy's acting styles (unhinged vs. contained), their characters' dialogue and their appearance, especially their clothing. Serge is often in a state of undress and wears dirty, work-soiled clothing with an old leather jacket. François, on the other hand, arrives at the guest house with neatly-folded shirts in his suitcase. He dresses like a dandy, and is often seen in polo neck sweaters and wearing a scarf. The stereotypes of the rugged, masculine outdoors type and his reserved, bookish and even prissy opposite are carefully contrived.

With its countryside setting, *Le Beau Serge* may come across as a rather odd New Wave film but Serge's alcoholism and François' spiritual crisis and apparent ambivalence to his future, set the template for a disenchanted post-war youth that would reappear in many a New Wave film to follow. *Le Beau Serge* also deals frankly with sexual relationships. Marie, the local 'alley cat,' lost her virginity at 15. She has slept with Serge and has a reputation as something of a man-eater. She and François share a casual sexual encounter (surprisingly initiated by the bashful-seeming François), which amounts to little afterward.

A born scene-stealer, Bernadette Lafont plays the part of Marie with a pouty, primal sexuality. Her raw performance is one of half a dozen potent turns. *Le Beau Serge* gains its strength from the quality of the acting. It's Brialy who really anchors the film, playing his part with true conviction, but you tend to remember Blain's hauntingly dishevelled, hangdog turn more clearly.

In-Jokes: Many of the extras and minor characters were played by the villagers of Sardent. Chabrol himself appears briefly as La Truffe. One of the characters, played by assistant director Philippe de Broca, is named Jacques Rivette.

The Verdict: Although a little rough around the edges, this is an exceptional achievement for a first-time director. Among the flashes of excellence are Serge's first appearance, accompanied by a discordant roar, and later, after a scuffle at a local dance, a haunting dissolve from François' bloody face to fresh falling snow. 4/5

Availability: VHS (Second Sight).

Now Try This: Chabrol's film is strongly influenced by Jacques Becker, who memorably evoked the lives of everyday people in features such as *Casque d'Or*.

Like Truffaut, Louis Malle was also quick to establish his own production company. From the late 1950s onwards, Nouvelles Editions De Films co-produced most of his features. After the success of *Ascenseur Pour L'Echafaud*, the director reunited with his lead actress, Jeanne Moreau, for *Les Amants*, another smart study of infidelity. Like *Et Dieu Créa la Femme*, the film was considered shocking at the time for its apparently loose morals and it became embroiled in a censorship debate. Unlike Vadim's movie, it still holds up today thanks to Malle's stylish and thoughtful treatment. Released in the same year as *Ascenseur Pour L'Echafaud*, the film went down a storm at the Venice Film Festival in 1959. It shared the Special Jury Prize with Francesco Rosi's *La Sfida* and sealed the director's reputation as an exciting new talent.

Les Amants (1958)

Alternative Title: *The Lovers*

Cast: Jeanne Moreau (Jeanne Tournier), Alain Cuny (Henri Tournier), Jean-Marc Bory (Bernard Dubois-Lambert), Judith Magre (Maggy Thiébaut-Leroy), José Luis de Villalonga (Raoul Flores), Gaston Modot (Coudray).

Crew: Directed by Louis Malle. Written by Louis Malle and Louise de Vilmorin. Based on the novel *Point de Lendemain* by Dominique Vivant, Baron de Denon. Produced by Irénée Leriche. Cinematography by Henri Decaë. Music by Johannes Brahms. 88 mins.

Story: Jeanne Tournier and Maggy Thiébaut-Leroy are childhood friends whose lives have taken different directions. The beautiful and bored Jeanne lives in a large, handsome house in Dijon with her husband, a newspaperman who is more interested in his job than his wife. She suspects that he is having an affair at work. After eight years of marriage they sleep in separate rooms. Maggy, who left Dijon when she was younger, has become a society girl in Paris. Jeanne finds comfort with Maggy and begins to stay with her most weekends. These liberating trips to Paris become more and more frequent, not least when she meets Raoul Flores, a dashing polo player who is considerably enamoured with her.

Growing suspicious of his wife's trips away, Jeanne's

husband bullies her into inviting Maggy and Raoul to come to Dijon for a meal, so that he can humiliate his wife and ensure that Raoul is put off the affair. The weekend takes an unexpected turn when Jeanne's car breaks down en route for home and she is forced to take a lift with Bernard, a younger stranger who she discovers is related to her high-society friends. Forced to spend the night with the Tourniers, Bernard opens the door to a new future for Jeanne after they spend a passionate night together.

Background: Narrated by an unnamed female, *Les Amants* slowly envelops the viewer as Malle takes his time setting the scene, carefully delineating his central characters and establishing a city/country dichotomy akin to *Le Beau Serge*. Jeanne Moreau, whose ability to yearn with such burning intensity is unmatched by any other actress, brilliantly conveys the sense of a woman suffocating in a stultifying marriage. Malle observes her prickly rifts with husband Henri, then juxtaposes them with the sense of excitement offered by the polo-playing Raoul, symbolised (a little too obviously) by the fairground ride they take together.

The film benefits from this languid pace, nowhere more so than the nocturnal, largely improvised interlude shared by Jeanne and Bernard, a sequence that stretches some 20 minutes involving, famously, one of the screen's first suggestions of cunnilingus. The film's international marketing campaign played upon the controversy surrounding these scenes, announcing *Les Amants* as "the most talked-about and fought-about film." Part of the shock was in seeing Jeanne kiss her daughter goodnight before heading next door to strip off with a virtual stranger.

Les Amants remains most interesting for this moonlight romance, during which Jeanne not only falls in love with Bernard but also with her countryside surroundings, previously forsaken for the delights of Paris. Taken individually, the elements seem ripe for ridicule. Our narrator informs us that "love can be born in a glance" while Bernard observes with assurance that "night is a woman." The pair cross stepping stones, catch fish and share an embrace in a boat. However, these scenes remain magically lyrical and tender. If Malle pulls it off, it's due in large part to his choice of Brahms as musical accompaniment and the gorgeous photography of Henri Decaë.

Continually dressed in a series of white outfits, Moreau illuminates the film. It's hard to imagine another actress doing justice to the part. Jeanne is perhaps her archetypal role, the woman who follows her instincts and refuses to hold regrets. In the other roles, Jean-Marc Bory makes a virile Bernard, Judith Magre preens with Parisian pretensions as Maggy and José Luis de Villalonga glows with catch-of-the-day pride as Raoul. Watch out for Claude Mansard too, as Henri's colleague at the newspaper. Mansard will later star as one of the gangsters in Truffaut's *Tirez Sur le Pianiste*.

The Verdict: Another impressively mature work from Malle, whose films consistently deliver third-act surprises. Intelligent and still powerfully erotic. 4/5

Availability: VHS (Electric Pictures), deleted.

Now Try This: Malle's 30th feature *Damage*, starring Juliette Binoche and Jeremy Irons, also examines marital disharmony and adultery. The film's sex scenes similarly sparked predictable press interest.

For his second film, shot shortly after *Le Beau Serge*, Chabrol again cast Jean-Claude Brialy and Gérard Blain in the lead roles. They are *Les Cousins*. These two films were released in close succession, which meant they played concurrently in theatres in a similar manner to Louis Malle's first films.

Les Cousins (1959)

Alternative Title: *The Cousins*

Cast: Gérard Blain (Charles), Jean-Claude Brialy (Paul), Juliette Mayniel (Florence), Guy Decomble (Bookseller), Geneviève Cluny (Geneviève), Michèle Méritz (Yvonne).

Crew: Directed by Claude Chabrol. Written by Claude Chabrol and Paul Gégauff. Produced by Claude Chabrol. Cinematography by Henri Decaë. Music by Paul Misraki. 105 mins.

Story: Charles, a young man from the country, arrives in Paris to study law. He stays with his pretentious cousin, Paul, a Mephistophelean character who is devoted to an extravagant lifestyle. Having driven him all around town, Paul takes Charles to his club, where the young Parisian-jet set play cards and flirt with each other. Charles is immediately attracted to Florence, one of his cousin's numerous female friends. After an evening of debauchery organised by Paul, Charles is delighted to receive a call from Florence. They arrange to meet up but, due to a misunderstanding, Florence arrives at Paul's apartment while Charles is still at college. Paul invites her in to wait and works hard to put a spanner in the works of Florence's blossoming relationship with his cousin. Within minutes they are sharing a passionate embrace. Almost as quickly, Florence has moved in, creating an impossible situation for Charles.

Background: This is a companion piece to Chabrol's first film. Watching the opening minutes of *Les Cousins* as the second half of a double bill with *Le Beau Serge* (the two are often screened together in repetition), it is hard to believe they came from the same director, let alone that they were made within such a short space of time of each other. The first picture's languid observations of a countryside community contrast dramatically with this film's snapshots of city living. The opening minutes of *Les Cousins*, in particular the sequence where Charles and Paul drive around Paris, promote the sense of freedom and excitement so often associated with the New Wave. Here, the viewer is placed in a glitzy city glimpsed in a similar manner to any number of 'swinging London' features of the 1960s.

Like *Le Beau Serge*, *Les Cousins* opens with an arrival and a reunion. The film then proceeds to effectively reverse the action of the earlier film. The outsider is this time played by Blain, who is unable to enter his cousin's social set, just as Brialy found it so difficult to re-enter the provincial community in the previous film. The focus is again the relationship between two men who find themselves involved in a love triangle. The characters are once more contrasted through language and costume. Paul has a decadent dress sense, while this time Blain's character is scrubbed up and looks like a mummy's boy. His close relationship with his mother is highlighted in the film through a series of letters home, revealing the feminine side of his nature in contrast to Paul's brash masculinity.

Brialy tucks into the role of Paul, a showman who loves to hold court and prides himself on his use of language. This time Blain shrinks inside himself as Charles who, from his opening conversation with the taxi driver onwards, is both reserved and prone to mistakes. Paul regularly brings attention to his cousin's rustic roots and Chabrol's film is full of subtle observations on urban and provincial lives. As in *Le Beau Serge*, characters can't help but pry into how the other half live. In one scene, Charles reveals his roots to a bookseller by confessing his love for Balzac; everyone in the city reads thrillers.

Les Cousins often feels exactly like what it is: the second film of a director afloat with the critical success and commercial revenue of his first picture. It exudes a certain sense of confidence that only a director at this stage of his career could display. The film's technical credits outweigh its predecessor. Henri Decaë's unfussy cinematography and Paul Misraki's score are particularly of note.

The Verdict: Although both leads turn in plum performances, the pace occasionally falters, the film feels too long and there's an absence at its heart, especially after the emotional impact of Chabrol's debut. Perhaps this hollowness stems from the overwhelming array of unsympathetic characters and their questionable pursuits. Charles is the only figure we warm to here. 3/5

Availability: VHS (Second Sight).

Now Try This: Federico Fellini's *La Dolce Vita*, released the following year, examines a similarly decadent and spiritually stunted society.

Les Cousins, like *Le Beau Serge*, was both a critical and a commercial success. The production company, set up by the young Chabrol, AJYM, went on to support the debut projects of Jacques Rivette and Eric Rohmer. Rohmer's first feature *Le Signe du Lion* was not only produced by Chabrol, but also featured a script by his friend and long-term collaborator Paul Gégauff. Rohmer's depiction of a summer that sees a change in the fortunes of its protagonist, a Bohemian musician named Pierre, has much in common with Chabrol's debut.

Le Signe du Lion (1959)

Alternative Title: *The Sign of Leo*

Cast: Jess Hahn (Pierre Wesselrin), Michèle Girardon (Dominique Laurent), Van Doude (Jean-François

Santeuil), Paul Bisciglia (Willy), Gilbert Edard (Michèle Caron).

Crew: Directed by Eric Rohmer. Written by Eric Rohmer and Paul Gégauff. Produced by Claude Chabrol and Roland Nonin. Cinematography by Nicolas Hayer. Music by Louis Saguer. 100 mins.

Story: "Merde!" Woken up by an insistent doorbell, penniless American Pierre answers his front door to receive a telegram bringing the news that his extremely wealthy aunt has died. Overjoyed, he immediately calls his friend Jean-François, to announce his forthcoming inheritance, which he believes merits a drinking binge for the evening. He swiftly rounds up a group of revellers to help him celebrate. However, three weeks later Pierre has seemingly disappeared and his friends search the city for him in vain. It is reported that he has not received the money he thought was coming his way.

Pierre is seen roaming the streets endlessly, stealing food and taking care to avoid his landlady, to whom he owes rent. Before long she catches up with him and his door keys are confiscated. Without a home, he is forced to contact his sparse number of friends, most of whom have left Paris for the summer, to find a bed for the night...

Background: Rohmer was 40 when he got his first feature made and the achievement owed much to the financial help of the *Cahiers* critics. Compared to the first films of Truffaut and Godard, *Le Signe du Lion* is undeniably hard work. Its heavy tone could be responsible for its commercial failure, which, compared to the ecstatic receptions of most of the New Wave films, must have hit Rohmer hard, especially after his long struggle to get it made in the first place.

Like the other New Wave films set in the capital, *Le Signe du Lion* revolves around a largely recognisable Paris. Several scenes take place in Saint-Germain-des-Prés and there is plenty of location shooting among the cafés. Paris is presented – perhaps more than in any other New Wave work – as a filthy and unattractive city, viewed through the eyes of the desperate and needy. As the lumbering, tragic figure of Pierre, Jess Hahn dominates the film, adding to the general air of gloom and emptiness with a performance of despair in the big city. The film is littered with painful moments. One of the most excruciating to sit through is one in which the tired and hungry Pierre rests on a bench next to three girls, who cheerfully discuss their fortunes and enjoy the refreshments he so clearly needs.

With its depiction of one man's long physical and spiritual decline, *Le Signe du Lion* recalls the great naturalist novels of Emile Zola as well as the works of American realists such as Theodore Dreiser. It marks Rohmer out as one of the most literary of New Wave directors, always devoting particular attention to his characters' inner thoughts. His later films would adopt a similar approach but usually have a lighter touch. The bizarre and beguiling *Le Genou de Claire* (1970), for example, concerns a man named Jerome (played by Jean-Claude Brialy) who becomes obsessed with the knee of a young girl while on holiday.

In-Jokes: Godard makes a brief appearance as the man sat next to the record player at the party in Pierre's flat.

The Verdict: If *The Lost Weekend* or *Leaving Las Vegas* is your idea of a good time at the movies, then give *Le Signe du Lion* a go. But you have been warned! The film's slow pace, piercing strings soundtrack and gruelling story make for a rather exhausting experience. 3/5

Availability: VHS (Hendrig), deleted.

Now Try This: Louis Malle treated similar themes in the haunting *Le Feu Follet* (1964), which follows a recovering alcoholic (Maurice Ronet) as he revisits old friends in Paris before committing suicide.

Cannes '59

François Truffaut was banned from the Cannes Film Festival in 1958 for the caustic remarks he had made about French cinema in his film criticism for *Cahiers*. On 10th November of that same year, using a small crew, he began to shoot his first feature film, *Les Quatre Cents Coups* (the title is idiomatic French for "raising merry hell"). *Cahiers* editor André Bazin died the very next day. The film was shot in less than two months and in 1959 Truffaut was in competition at Cannes with the finished film, which he dedicated to the memory of Bazin.

Les Quatre Cents Coups (1959)

Alternative Title: *The 400 Blows*

Cast: Jean-Pierre Léaud (Antoine Doinel), Claire Maurier (Mme Doinel), Albert Rémy (M Doinel), Guy Decomble (Schoolmaster), Patrick Auffay (René Bigey), Georges Flamant (M Bigey), Yvonne Claudie (Mme Bigey), Claude Mansard (Judge).

Crew: Directed by François Truffaut. Written by François Truffaut and Marcel Moussy. Produced by

Georges Charlot. Cinematography by Henri Decaë.
Music by Jean Constantin. 95 mins.

Story: Antoine Doinel studies at a grim boys' school
and lives in a cramped apartment with his irritable
mother and more genial stepfather. He spends the
nights on the floor in a sleeping bag, kept awake by
their arguments. The morning after a typically horrific
day at school, Antoine and his friend René bunk off to
go to the cinema and the funfair. Their day is spoilt
when Antoine spies his mother embracing a stranger.
This betrayal is surely in his head the next day when, in
need of an excuse for his absence, he tells his teacher his
mother is dead.

The news ricochets to Antoine's parents and Antoine
leaves home but, after an unhappy night spent in an old
printing works, he returns to his family. The family then
enjoys a momentarily idyllic period, during which time
they go to the cinema, but then Antoine and René try
to get some quick cash by stealing a typewriter from
Antoine's stepfather's office. Antoine is caught, charged
and placed in an observation centre for juvenile delinquents. But it will take more than this to keep the irrepressible kid down.

Background: Truffaut once aligned a director's oeuvre
to a life-long diary and his first feature is one from the
heart, notable for its highly autobiographical nature. It
was no secret that the character of Antoine Doinel, as
played in a total of five films by Jean-Pierre Léaud,
grew from Truffaut's own childhood. Léaud and Doinel
became cinematic alter-egos for the director. *Les Quatre*

Cents Coups was shot on the same streets where Truffaut had grown up and there's a strong sense of his instinctive feel for the locations. Several of the scenes in the Doinel films were directly inspired by events in Truffaut's own life. Like Antoine, he was forced to sleep in the corridor of his family's cramped apartment. He ran away from home on more than one occasion and was also placed in an observation centre for delinquents.

Truffaut's best friend Robert Lachenay was the inspiration for the character of René, Antoine's partner in crime, played here by Patrick Auffay. The conspiratorial relationship between René and Antoine is especially convincing. The pair share a touching alliance, represented best by the moving scene in which René attempts to visit his friend in the institution. Auffay's is one of many fine, naturalistic supporting turns. Truffaut skilfully handles another crop of badly behaved 'mistons' and he also draws sterling work from Albert Rémy and Claire Maurier, as Antoine's parents, and Guy Decomble as the stern professor. All three veer between displays of animosity and affection for Antoine.

At the heart of the film is a towering lead performance from the young Léaud, who brings a high level of humanity to Antoine's sullen swagger. One moment impenetrable and indifferent, the next helpless, Léaud gives an impressively complex turn as a boy who seems older than his years. He drives the film, appearing in virtually every scene. His performance evokes the full range of childhood emotions, from overwhelming youthful passions (Antoine's are, like Truffaut's, for the cinema and literature) to disillusionment with one's lot in life.

Les Quatre Cents Coups is a celebration of the giddy liberty of youth, represented by the film's freewheeling opening, Antoine and René's sprints through the streets (to the sound of Jean Constantin's twinkly score) and in particular Antoine's spin on a fairground ride. However, the film also reinforces the crushing confines of childhood, represented by the family's claustrophobic apartment and the school's barren classroom, both of which anticipate the cell Antoine ends up in. The manner of Antoine's education itself comes under attack, damned as a dreary series of recitations and dictations.

This invigorating film immediately established Truffaut as the French New Wave's most commercially successful director. It was awarded the Director's Prize at Cannes, received an Oscar® nomination for its script and signalled Truffaut's arrival on the international scene. Akira Kurosawa championed the picture as "one of the most beautiful films that I have ever seen" and Jacques Rivette described it in *Cahiers* as 'a triumph of simplicity.' From this point onwards, the New Wave could not be ignored.

In-Jokes: There are cameo appearances from a host of New Wave stars. Truffaut himself appears in the funfair scene, while director Jacques Demy plays a policeman. In cameo appearances, Jeanne Moreau plays a woman chasing a dog and Jean-Claude Brialy steps in to offer his assistance. Jean Douchet stars as Mme Doinel's lover. When Antoine goes to the cinema with his family, they see Jacques Rivette's *Paris Nous Appartient*. Antoine and

René also steal a still of Harriet Andersson in *Summer with Monika*.

The Verdict: From the lyrical opening shots of the Eiffel Tower to the famous enigmatic freeze frame with which it ends, the film sports inspired direction from Truffaut. Both perceptive and poignant, it still feels impressively fresh and the timeless nature of its story means audiences of all ages and generations can empathise with it. 5/5

Availability: Region 2 DVD (Tartan) includes Truffaut's short film *Les Mistons* and original trailers. VHS (Artificial Eye) also includes *Les Mistons* but is deleted.

Now Try These: Jean-Pierre Léaud plays Antoine Doinel in four more films: *Antoine et Colette, Baisers Volés, Domicile Conjugal* and *L'Amour en Fuite*.

1959 was to prove a banner year for the French New Wave. Truffaut's success at Cannes was one part of French cinema's three-pronged victory at the festival. Marcel Camus' *Orfeu Negro* (*Black Orpheus*), a reworking of the popular Orpheus and Eurydice story, took home the Palme d'Or and Alain Resnais won the International Critics' Prize for his first feature film *Hiroshima Mon Amour*, which was shown out of competition. Resnais had, by this time, already made a name for himself as a documentary film-maker, with short portraits of painters (*Van Gogh* and *Gauguin*) and the devastating Holocaust documentary *Nuit et Brouillard*.

A 30-minute collage which was filmed in colour and also featured black and white photographs and newsreel footage, *Nuit et Brouillard* focused on the Nazi concentration camps of the Second World War and displayed the influence of Sergei Eisenstein's celebrated montage sequences. Using a narrative text written by a survivor of Mauthausen and read by Michel Bouquet (*La Femme Infidèle*), the film cut seamlessly between the sites of the concentration camps today and the horrors that they housed during the war. A truly harrowing history lesson told with dramatic panache, Resnais' documentary won the Prix Jean Vigo and prefigured *Hiroshima Mon Amour* by employing newsreel material and creatively interweaving the past and present.

Hiroshima Mon Amour (1959)

Alternative Title: *Hiroshima My Love*

Cast: Emmanuelle Riva (Elle), Eiji Okada (Lui), Stella Dassus (Mother), Pierre Barbaud (Father), Bernard Fresson (German Lover).

Crew: Directed by Alain Resnais. Written by Marguerite Duras. Produced by Anatole Dauman, Samy Halfon, Sacha Kamenka and Takeo Shirakawa. Cinematography by Michio Takahashi and Sacha Vierny. Music by Georges Delerue and Giovanni Fusco. 86 mins.

Story: Summer, 1957. Hiroshima. A French actress from Paris, in Japan to make an international film on peace, meets and shares a brief and passionate affair with a Japanese architect. The woman, whose name we never learn, is set to return to France the day after she meets the Japanese man, who remains similarly anonymous. Both are married with children. Both have other lives. However, they are impossibly drawn to one another. As time passes, these lovers from very different backgrounds struggle to understand not only each other, but also each other's culture.

Background: The New Wave's innovative approach to film-making was paralleled in the literary world of the 1950s by the explosion of the so-called New Novel (*nouveau roman*). Writers like Alain Robbe-Grillet and Claude Simon broke new boundaries with fiction, just as the *Cahiers* critics did with film. Alain Resnais, like Chris Marker and Agnès Varda, drew inspiration from the New Novel and produced a series of films whose influences are perhaps as literary as they are cinematic. For *Hiroshima Mon Amour*, Resnais collaborated with acclaimed author Marguerite Duras whose dazzling, Oscar®-nominated screenplay frequently borders on the poetic.

Resnais' treatment of time in *Hiroshima Mon Amour* is considered revolutionary for film art. He changed the way we perceive time on screen and, to fully comprehend his achievement, we have to take a lead from his heroine who says, "It's my idea that we see nothing without being willing to struggle to learn the way to see." Resnais' intelligent use of time is multi-layered. For example, time is running out for the couple from the film's very opening as the woman is set to leave the city. More importantly, the narrative switches seamlessly between current and historical events. The way in which different eras bleed into one another here also recalls the novels of Bloomsbury writer Virginia Woolf and Irish author James Joyce. Resnais' rejection of conventional narrative structure would later be echoed in the work of Godard, who famously commented that every film must have a beginning, a middle and an end, although not necessarily in that order.

"The past and the present coexist," Resnais told *Interview* in November 1999, "but the past shouldn't be in flashback. The heroine's memory, her affair with the German soldier, was the past, but the sound was in the present; we hear the sounds of Tokyo." As Resnais' film moves between past and present, it combines a number of other opposites: war and peace, past and present, reality and memory, private and public, life and death, madness and sanity, truth and lies, romance and horror.

There are other opposites at play, namely documentary and fiction, memorably blended together in the film's opening minutes. Resnais' documentary background is very much on display in this enthralling sequence; a dazzling collage detailing the horrors of Hiroshima in much the same fashion as *Nuit et Brouillard* dealt with the Holocaust. Resnais patrols the halls of a Hiroshima museum, picking out exhibits with the same unflinching eye. The comb made by a concentration camp prisoner in the earlier film, here finds its match with a clump of human hair shed from a Hiroshima victim.

Hiroshima Mon Amour amounts to a two-hander and Emmanuelle Riva and Eiji Okada deliver strong performances, veering between sensuousness and seriousness. Riva, appearing in her first picture, skilfully handles the bulk of the dialogue. The film is also technically excellent. The use of light is consistently striking, especially during the lovers' intimate liaisons indoors and the woman's harrowing cave memories. The editing astonishes throughout, notably in the beginning but also during the woman's recollections of a youthful romance. Meanwhile, Georges Delerue and Giovanni Fusco's score covers a clutter of contradictory emotions and is intermittently sprightly, mournful, disturbing and deeply beautiful.

In-Jokes: The couple spend their last hours together in a bar called Casablanca. Coincidence or homage?

The Verdict: Resnais proved his directorial dexterity with this groundbreaking and enigmatic brief encounter. A landmark in French cinema, *Hiroshima Mon Amour* offers both a challenging and rewarding experience. 4/5

Availability: VHS (Nouveau Pictures) and Region 2 DVD (Nouveau Pictures) including documentary.

Now Try This: Resnais' next film, *L'Année Dernière à Marienbad*, is another study of time and memory.

Guns, Girls and Gauloises

Back in 1956 François Truffaut had written a brief treatment for a crime film inspired by a news story, but the project was sidelined while he made *Les Quatre Cents Coups*. After the surprise success of his debut feature, he began to develop other films and passed his original treatment on to Godard, who decided to use it as the basis for his own debut, *A Bout de Souffle*. Godard fleshed out Truffaut's treatment, expanding some of the scenes and significantly changing the ending. The film was then shot entirely on location at the end of summer in 1959.

For the main role, Truffaut had considered Jean-Claude Brialy or Gérard Blain. Instead, Godard cast unconventional leading man Jean-Paul Belmondo, the son of sculptor Paul Belmondo. Belmondo junior had trained as a boxer before studying at the Conservatoire in Paris. He had already appeared in some of Godard's early shorts, such as *Charlotte et Son Jules*, which is considered a dry run for the director's first feature.

A Bout de Souffle (1959)

Alternative Title: *Breathless*

Cast: Jean-Paul Belmondo (Michel Poiccard, alias Laszlo Kovacs), Jean Seberg (Patricia Franchini), Daniel Boulanger (Inspector Vital), Henri-Jacques Huet (Antonio Berruti), Roger Hanin (Carl Zombach), Jean-Pierre Melville (Parvulesco).

Crew: Directed by Jean-Luc Godard. Written by Jean-Luc Godard and François Truffaut. Produced by Georges de Beauregard. Cinematography by Raoul Coutard. Music by Martial Solal. 90 mins.

Story: A tall man stands in the shadows of a Marseilles street reading a paper. Wearing a baggy, crumpled suit, with hat cocked and fag in mouth, Michel Poiccard seems almost American yet remains impossibly Gallic. Within seconds, he has stolen a car and is heading for Paris. En route to the capital he discovers a handgun in the glove compartment. With his gangster outfit complete, he plays at being a hood, aiming the gun out of the car window. When two policemen appear in his rear-view mirror, Michel veers off the road and no longer acts the role. He shoots one of the policemen dead then hotfoots it across the countryside.

Michel reaches Paris and hooks up with Patricia, an American student who sells copies of the *New York Herald Tribune* along the Champs Elysées. Michel has come to Paris for two reasons: to reclaim some money from an acquaintance and to persuade Patricia to accompany him to Italy. Chain-smoking Gauloises and determined to live dangerously, his time in the city slowly runs out, as the police catch up with him when he is betrayed by his girlfriend.

Background: Directed by Godard from a treatment by Truffaut and made with 'artistic and technical advice' from Chabrol, *A Bout de Souffle* is for many the quintessential New Wave film. The story of its production is steeped in cinematic myth. Famously, Godard made corrections to the script right up until the last minute, whispering the lines to the actors. For the tracking shots, he pushed cameraman Raoul Coutard around Paris in a wheelchair, in order to save money on customary pieces of equipment. A former photojournalist, Coutard worked with Godard on several of his acclaimed 1960s features, as did actor Belmondo who became the New Wave's king of cool and enjoyed roles in both *Une Femme est Une Femme* and *Pierrot le Fou.*

A Bout de Souffle set the mould for the New Wave more than its precedents, not only in terms of its cast and crew, but also in its rebellious style and attitude and its visual and narrative virtuosity. The film captures the New Wave's revolt against traditional forms of cinematic storytelling. Godard refuses to play the game of traditional Hollywood cinema and this is shown right from the start, as he skips the traditional title sequence, opening instead – like Malle's *Ascenseur Pour L'Echafaud* – with an extreme close-up.

A Bout de Souffle is as stylistically complex as its plot is simple. All the commonly perceived hallmarks of the New Wave can be found here: cine-literacy and homage, young and sexy stars, visually arresting jump-cuts, loose hand-held camerawork, an improvised jazz score, quirky humour, dialogue spoken direct to the camera and abrupt changes of pace and mood. *Variety*'s reviewer, in January 1960, found it a "grabbag mixture of content, satire, drama and protest" and reported that, "Characters suddenly shift around rooms, have different bits of clothing on within two shots, etc. But all this seems acceptable for this unorthodox film moves quickly and ruthlessly."

There's also the familiar use of real and recognisable locations such as the Champs Elysées and Orly airport. As Truffaut had with *Les Quatre Cents Coups*, Godard shot the film on the streets he knew. "This documentary interest in places comes from the Nouvelle Vague," he told *Film Comment* in a 2005 interview concerning *Notre Musique*. "One of the things that bothered us in the French "tradition of quality" films was the complete lack of interest in places, which were neither understood nor looked at. When I put Belmondo and Jean Seberg on the Champs-Elysées, it was because I walked up that avenue every day."

Godard's debut is a French film soaked in Americana. Iowa-born actress Jean Seberg, who appeared in Otto Preminger's *Saint Joan*, is an American in Paris who sells an American newspaper. Michel's favourite actor is Humphrey Bogart and improvised jazz forms part of the film's soundtrack. Belmondo cuts the appearance of an American gangster and his character has reminiscences of the lone cowboy. *A Bout de Souffle* also recalls the many American lovers-on-the-lam movies made in the 1950s, such as Joseph H Lewis' *Gun Crazy*. As an affectionate homage to the B-movies of the American studio Monogram Pictures, the film foreshadows the director's later homage to the American musical (*Une Femme est Une Femme*).

The film's relationship to the crime genre is an interesting one. Godard commented that when he started out he intended *A Bout de Souffle* to be a realistic slice of film noir, but when he was finished he thought it was more like *Alice in Wonderland*. The truth lies somewhere in-between. Although we are constantly aware that Michel plays the role of a criminal (or rather, Belmondo plays the role of Michel who plays the role of Bogart), many of the scenes are nevertheless chilling. Like Michel, who performs his chicaneries with a likeable smile, the film also has the power to charm. *A Bout de Souffle* reflects Godard's later pictures through its use of a simple story, as the backdrop for some entertaining lovers' debate. The thriller plot is left to simmer in a lengthy change-of-pace scene that takes up roughly one third of the film, Patricia and Michel potter around her apartment, play records, muse over the arts, contemplate philosophical theories of freedom and play a series of tender games.

Like Truffaut and Chabrol's first features, *A Bout de Souffle* was instantly revered upon its release. It was awarded the Prix Jean Vigo and the Silver Bear for Best Director at the Berlin Film Festival. The trendsetting nature of the picture ranged from cinema to fashion, as women rushed out to copy Jean Seberg's sexy cropped cut.

In-Jokes: *Hiroshima Mon Amour* is playing at a local

cinema. A young girl tries to sell Michel a copy of *Cahiers*. Godard makes a cameo appearance as the informer. Director Jean-Pierre Melville stars as the novelist Parvulesco, whom Patricia interviews on a rooftop by Orly airport. Michel's trademark tic of wiping his lips with the tip of his thumb comes from Bogart's performance in *The Maltese Falcon*, while his death recalls Bogart's demise in *High Sierra*. Godard commented that the character of Patricia Franchini was a continuation of Seberg's role in Otto Preminger's *Bonjour Tristesse*.

The Verdict: It's hard to imagine the history of cinema without *A Bout de Souffle*. An irresistible and essential work, it repays any number of repeat viewings. 5/5

Availability: VHS (Optimum) and Region 2 DVD (Optimum) with poster gallery, stills, trailers for the original and the US remake, production notes and Godard's earlier short, *Charlotte et Son Jules*, starring Belmondo, Gérard Blain and Anne Colette.

Now Try These: The film was updated to the streets of Los Angeles in Jim McBride's best-avoided *Breathless* (1983), starring a frilly-shirted, comic book-loving Richard Gere. Toby MacDonald's BAFTA-nominated short *Je T'Aime John Wayne* (2000) is an affectionate and amusing spoof starring *Love Actually*'s Kris Marshall.

Within a year of the appearance of both *A Bout de Souffle* and *Les Quatre Cents Coups*, Truffaut's own unconventional take on the crime genre, *Tirez Sur le*

Pianiste, was released to the praise of critics, although not – if box-office receipts are anything to go by – the general public. For his second full-length feature, Truffaut chose to adapt a short novel by unsung American crime writer David Goodis and collaborated once more with Marcel Moussy on the screenplay.

Entitled *Down There,* the original novel covered typical Goodis territory and was set in the seedier regions of the author's home town of Philadelphia. Truffaut had read the novel shortly after finishing his treatment for *A Bout de Souffle* and he quickly devoured everything Goodis had written. Elements of several of the author's other novels, therefore, found themselves drawn into the artistic patchwork of *Tirez Sur le Pianiste.*

Tirez Sur le Pianiste (1960)

Alternative Titles: *Shoot the Piano Player, Shoot the Pianist*

Cast: Charles Aznavour (Charlie Kohler/Edouard Saroyan), Marie Dubois (Léna), Nicole Berger (Thérésa), Michèle Mercier (Clarisse), Serge Davri (Plyne), Claude Mansard (Momo), Richard Kanayan (Fido), Albert Rémy (Chico).

Crew: Directed by François Truffaut. Written by François Truffaut and Marcel Moussy. Based on the novel *Down There* by David Goodis. Produced by Pierre Braunberger. Cinematography by Raoul Coutard. Music by Georges Delerue. 82 mins.

Story: Chico runs frantically down an alley in an anonymous French town. It is dark. So dark in fact, that he runs straight into a lamp-post and is knocked down. He's helped to his feet by a passer-by and then continues to run until he finds a lively bar. Here he meets his brother, the bar's laconic pianist, who he hasn't seen for years. His brother seems unthrilled to see him, especially as Chico explains that he is in trouble and needs help. The pianist knows trouble like the back of his hand. A childhood prodigy and one-time concert pianist, he is haunted by the memories of his wife's suicide and now makes ends meet playing honky-tonk to an unappreciative audience of bums and drunkards.

As two men enter the bar searching for his brother, the pianist aids his getaway. When he wakes up the following morning, and sees the two men outside his bedroom window, it becomes clear that he hasn't heard the last of the matter. Chico's misdemeanours have brought him into a dangerous situation in which both the pianist and the woman he grows to love will find themselves trapped.

Background: Like Godard, Truffaut chose to make *Tirez Sur le Pianiste* partly to show his debt to American B-movies and pulp fiction. His second film was also a kind of reaction against his first. The director had been projected to great fame as the creator of *Les Quatre Cents Coups*, yet wasn't afraid to say that the acclaim of the general public (those viewers who watch perhaps just one or two movies a year) meant little to him. He decided that his next film wouldn't concern childhood and would be a step away from sentimentality. It would be a film for the film buffs, full of in-jokes and allusions that his friends at *Cahiers* would recognise. Above all, it would be a feature for himself and a good deal of fun to make.

Many of the noir touches of Goodis' original novel remain in the film, such as the dark alleyways and lowlife locations, all memorably shot by *A Bout de Souffle* cinematographer Raoul Coutard. As in the original novel (which opens with the line 'There were no street lamps, no lights at all'), darkness pervades Truffaut's film. Aznavour's pianist is a typical noir hero. Living in temporary accommodation and dogged by a tragic past, he doesn't give anything away or let anyone in. As is remarked in both the film and the novel, the pianist usually walks alone, 'even when he's with someone.' Like Michel Poiccard and Antoine Doinel, he is marginalised and misunderstood, an anti-hero.

As well as maintaining the dark and dramatic atmosphere of his source material, Truffaut plays with a number of different genres in the film, so that it becomes a mixture of the romance, comedy, melodrama and tragedy genres, as well as a crime picture. It is the film's abundant comic touches in particular that distinguish it from the novel. Some of the early scenes in Plyne's bar are especially humorous and there is some gentle comedy in the sequence where Charlie walks alongside Léna and tries to hold her hand. Truffaut plays up the romance element of the story and softens the hard guys, who at one point have a discussion about musical lighters and other toys. The film is famous for the comic scene, where one of the gangsters proclaims "May my mother drop dead if I tell a lie", to which

Truffaut replies with a shot of an old woman collapsing.

Such generic playfulness and swift changes of mood make *Tirez Sur le Pianiste* particularly hard to pin down and the film's publicists stressed this fact. The original trailers stated that the film "plays in many keys – all of them delightful, all of them different." Through using in these diverse keys, the film essentially subverts the original gangster genre in a similar manner to *A Bout de Souffle*.

In-Jokes: The pianist's brother, Chico (played by Albert Rémy, Antoine Doinel's father in *Les Quatre Cents Coups*), is named after one of the Marx Brothers. One of the gangsters is called Momo, which was Eric Rohmer's nickname. There is an advert for *Cahiers* on the back of a truck. In a typically self-conscious New Wave scene, Aznavour covers up a nude woman with a sheet, claiming "this is what they do in the movies."

The Verdict: Criminally overlooked on its initial release, this remains one of Truffaut's finest works. Made with great gusto, it's an irreverent and exhilarating work. 5/5

Availability: VHS (Artificial Eye), deleted.

Now Try These: Many of Goodis' stories of drink and downfall have been adapted for the big screen. *Dark Passage* was made into a film by Delmer Daves starring Bogart and Bacall. Much of his fiction is no longer in print, but *Down There* is currently available (repackaged as *Shoot the Piano Player*), as are *The Blonde on the Street Corner* and *Nightfall*.

Les Femmes

Having made two stylish black and white dramas, both starring Jeanne Moreau and both dealing with adultery, Louis Malle may have been in danger of becoming a predictable director. To anyone who believed as much, his third film proved a comprehensive shock to the system. Based on a 1959 novel by poet, essayist and scriptwriter Raymond Queneau, *Zazie Dans le Métro* is an exuberant, provocative and surreal farce painted in a vivid, vibrant palette. (It's Malle's first colour film.) The picture, which was initially to have been made by René Clément, immediately gave Malle a reputation as a versatile creative force. Here he directs with a sense of abandon, breaking free from the controlled tone of his first films.

Zazie Dans le Métro (1960)

Alternative Titles: *Zazie, Zazie in the Subway, Zazie in the Underground*

Cast: Catherine Demongeot (Zazie), Philippe Noiret (Uncle Gabriel), Odette Piquet (Zazie's Mother), Nicolas Bataille (Fedor), Antoine Roblot (Charles), Carla Marlier (Albertine).

Crew: Directed by Louis Malle. Written by Louis Malle and Jean-Paul Rappeneau. Based on the novel *Zazie Dans le Métro* by Raymond Queneau. Produced by Louis Malle. Cinematography by Henri Raichi. Music by Fiorenzo Carpi and André Pontin. 88 mins.

Story: An 11-year-old provincial girl, Zazie, arrives in Paris with her mother and is quickly passed on to her uncle Gabriel at the station, while her mum spends time with her fancy man. New to Paris, Zazie has one desire: to ride on the metro. However, a workers' strike makes this impossible and turns her uncle's weekend into a nightmare, as his admirably foul-mouthed niece creates havoc across the city and embroils him in a plot that will include chorus girls, food fights, traffic jams, kidnapping and a memorable talking parrot.

Background: That *Zazie Dans le Métro* could have been made by the same director as *Les Amants* is surprising even now, for Malle has swapped the subtleties of his mature relationship dramas for a manic, haphazard comedy. As he had already proved in his earlier films, he is a master of pace and it is to his credit that he manages to keep up the frenetic tempo of the opening minutes throughout the whole film. Watching *Zazie Dans le Métro* is akin to entering a cartoon or a comic strip as the viewer is sucked into an unpredictable world that has its own rules. In the chase scenes, Zazie and her uncle adopt the roles of Tom and Jerry or, more appropriately considering the dynamite explosions, the roadrunner and Wile E Coyote. Malle uses a host of anarchic, whirlwind effects, many of which are borrowed from the exaggerated farces of the silent era and raucous music hall entertainments. Slapstick therefore runs alongside grand musical routines, during which characters dress up in elaborate costumes. Malle relies on jagged editing and jump-cuts in particular to catch the viewer (and Zazie's unfortunate uncle) off balance.

Like *A Bout de Souffle*, *Zazie Dans le Métro* was shot on location in Paris and the two films have a lot in common, not least in the way they play with language. Both are a nightmare for subtitlers, as Zazie and Michel share eccentric dialects that are difficult to translate successfully. Interestingly, both Michel and Zazie also have a love for all things American. Michel's fondness for American cars and crime films parallels Zazie's love of Coca-Cola and her desire for a pair of blue jeans. By using elements of musicals, comic strips and cartoons, Malle also subverts American genres in a similar fashion to Godard.

As a celebration of youth and rebellion, *Zazie Dans le Métro* is of course a typical New Wave picture. The noisy girl in the orange sweater (played, amazingly, by a non-professional actress appearing in front of a camera for the first time) is an enduring symbol of irrepressible energy. "These modern children. No respect for their elders," comments Zazie's uncle, immediately showing himself up as the disgruntled 'cinéma de papa,' put out by the New Wave youth explosion.

In-Jokes: "Screw the New Wave," cries Zazie to anyone who will listen. "Screw you," says Malle to the New Wave's increasing number of detractors.

The Verdict: A true one-off, the madcap *Zazie Dans le Métro* remains an invigorating, dizzying experience. It's a little uneven but there are more hits than misses here. 3/5

Availability: VHS (Electric Pictures), deleted.

Now Try These: Queneau wrote the scripts for several films, including Alain Resnais' *Le Chant du Styrène*. He also appeared in Claude Chabrol's *Landru*.

Like Louis Malle, Claude Chabrol also reacted against his previous work with his 1960 release *Les Bonnes Femmes*. His first two films, *Le Beau Serge* and *Les Cousins*, had displayed a strong masculine bias, as had his third and most expensive yet, *A Double Tour* (1959), an adaptation of a crime novel by Stanley Ellin. For his fourth, he assembled a strong female cast including Bernadette Lafont and Stéphane Audran, who had played a minor role in *Les Cousins*.

Les Bonnes Femmes (1960)

Alternative Titles: *The Girls, The Good Girls*

Cast: Stéphane Audran (Ginette), Bernadette Lafont (Jane), Clotilde Joano (Jacqueline), Lucile Saint-Simon (Rita).

Crew: Directed by Claude Chabrol. Written by Claude Chabrol and Paul Gégauff. Produced by Ralph Baum and Charles L Bitsch. Cinematography by Henri Decaë. Music by Pierre Jansen and Paul Misraki. 93 mins.

Story: Outside the Grisbi club in the small hours of the morning, a bunch of revellers spill onto the streets and head for home. Two of them, the fun-loving Jane and the timid Jacqueline, are followed by a couple of older gentlemen, Albert and Marcel, who succeed in persuading them to go to a restaurant. After a raucous evening, Jacqueline goes home while Jane spends the night at Albert's apartment with both men. In the morning, she returns to her own apartment, where she lives with Ginette, a disillusioned friend who works in the same shop as her.

They arrive at work tired but on time, unlike Jacqueline who is starting at the shop that very day and is slightly late. The girls' odious boss takes pleasure in reprimanding her. With the fourth shop assistant Rita, the girls watch the clock by day and drink by night. Jane is enjoying an on-off relationship with an amicable soldier, while Rita is enamoured with the prim and proper Henri. Meanwhile, Jacqueline is intrigued by a mysterious motorcyclist who always seems to be around, and Ginette keeps a secret from the group.

Background: With *Les Bonnes Femmes*, Chabrol displays a masterly control of contrasting tones, balancing the film's amusing scenes with a dark undercurrent of tension, first announced in the music for the title sequence which leaves the viewer feeling uneasy throughout. Chabrol has always excelled at establishing a certain mood early on in his films. The opening scene captures this tonal range. There's much mirth in the goofiness of Albert and Marcel's predatory pursuit of Jane and Jacqueline but you're never quite sure whether their boozy evening will end in laughter or tears – especially when the drunken Jane is left alone with the men. The same doubt applies to the character of the motorcyclist who lurks in the shadows and then slides into Jacqueline's life. Will he prove friend or foe?

Other episodes in the film are more broadly humorous. Chabrol observes the film's party sequences in a similar manner to *Les Cousins* – witness the Felliniesque excesses of the nightclub Jane and Jacqueline visit with their older admirers. The scene in which a nervous and highly-strung Henri prepares his girlfriend Rita for the arrival of his overbearing parents is especially hilarious. He quizzes her on art and culture with an air of desperation, as they approach their table in the restaurant. The film is also punctuated with disturbing and downright bizarre sequences, such as when the elderly woman in the shop shows her unsavoury lucky charm to the fragile Jacqueline.

The rhythms of this beguiling film are those of the working week. The girls yawn their way through the days in the shop and wring as much amusement as possible out of their spare time, much like Juliete Hardy did in *Et Dieu Créa la Femme*. Chabrol, like Vadim, deftly depicts the gulf between his young protagonists and the older generation of characters (the shop owner, the girls' boss, Henri's parents), who are largely disapproving eccentrics with outmoded attitudes. Chabrol goes further by distinguishing the differing situations of the girls themselves, from Rita's tentative steps towards an inevitable-seeming marriage to the way Jane plays the field.

Les Bonnes Femmes was Chabrol's second successive

commercial failure and heralded a box-office slump in his career. "When I finished *Les Bonnes Femmes*, I was so proud," he told *Films in Review* in 1990. "Friends cried and kissed me. When I went to a screening, I was sure there would be thunderous applause. After ten minutes, people began to whistle. When they left the theatre, they drove away most of the people who had come for the next showing."

In-Jokes: Chabrol makes a cameo appearance in the film as a client in a café.

The Verdict: The film remains an intriguing oddity although the ending doesn't pack the punch it perhaps needs. It's worth a watch for the performances of the 'bonnes femmes' themselves, particularly the sparky Lafont and the muted Joano, whose neatly contrasting acting styles directly recall Blain and Brialy's work in the earlier films. 3/5

Availability: Region 1 DVD (Kino).

Now Try This: *Les Biches* is another female-focused drama starring Audran.

The undisputed romantic hero of the French New Wave was Jacques Demy who, throughout his lengthy career, created a number of luminous fables influenced by classic Hollywood musicals. His first film, *Lola*, was a tribute to Max Ophüls, who died in 1957, and to his influential picture *Lola Montès* (1955). It was produced by former journalist Georges de Beauregard, who produced Godard's first features and *Cléo de 5 à 7*, the debut of Demy's wife, Agnès Varda. Demy's films are characteristically set in seaside towns and ports. Born in Pont-Château, he had studied art in Nantes and it was here that he decided to film *Lola*.

Lola (1960)

Cast: Anouk Aimée (Lola), Marc Michel (Roland), Elina Labourdette (Madame Desnoyers), Alan Scott (Frankie), Annie Duperoux (Cécile), Jacques Harden (Michel).

Crew: Directed and written by Jacques Demy. Produced by Georges de Beauregard and Carlo Ponti. Cinematography by Raoul Coutard. Music by Michel Legrand. (Song 'Moi j'étais pour elle' by Marguerite Monnot, 'C'est moi, c'est Lola' written by Agnès Varda). 91 mins.

Story: Roland and Lola are childhood friends who haven't seen one another for 15 years. A chance encounter brings them back together. Their lives have changed immeasurably. Roland has become disillusioned since the war. With his nose constantly in a book and his head in the clouds, he has gone through a series of menial and unsatisfying jobs. The day he meets Lola he is sacked for poor timekeeping. Lola, on the other hand, has a young son from a brief affair with a man who left her when she became pregnant. In the seven years since he left, she has worked hard to support herself and her child. She is now a popular cabaret artist. Roland and Lola's chance meeting is the first of several encounters and reunions in the film.

Background: 'Weep who may, laugh who will,' proclaims the Chinese proverb which opens the film. It is a telling proverb not only for *Lola*, but for Demy's work in general. Like his later feature, *Les Parapluies de Cherbourg*, *Lola* tells a tale of unwanted pregnancy, employment struggles, the pain of absence and the failure of childhood romances. However, it is told in such a breezy fashion that the viewer is won over by the picture's sheer *joie de vivre*. Alongside George Cukor and Pedro Almodóvar, Demy was one of cinema's greatest directors of women. With *Lola* he extracted a bewitching, BAFTA-nominated performance from Aimée who dashes from scene to scene, all lashes, curls and mile-wide smile. She embodies the exuberance and optimism that the film exudes.

Like both Godard and Truffaut, Demy was strongly influenced by American movies. The look and tone of his film were influenced by the musicals of Ernst Lubitsch. The world of Nantes and the film itself are infiltrated by Americana — witness the mysterious cigar-chewing, Stetson-wearing figure in the opening scene. Lola's liaison with the American sailor, Frankie, mirrors Michel and Patricia's romance in *A Bout de Souffle*. The port sees a never-ending influx of such sailors looking for fun, bringing to mind musicals like *On the Town*. The opening of Demy's third film, *Les Parapluies de Cherbourg*, would find the characters literally 'singin' in the rain'.

In-Jokes: "Life's always nice in films," one of the characters comments. Roland refers to *A Bout de Souffle* when he remarks that his friend Poiccard was shot by the police. You get the feeling that Roland wishes he could be like the hero of Godard's debut. Roland spends his days – not unlike the *Cahiers* critics – at the local cinema, watching American movies such as the Gary Cooper picture *Return to Paradise*. Lola takes inspiration for her outfits from Marilyn Monroe.

The Verdict: Carried by Michel Legrand's lush score, this is a dazzling debut. There's some diamond-smuggling shenanigans going on in the background but *Lola* is for the most part a thoughtful meditation on relationships both old and new. 3/5

Availability: Region 1 DVD (Wellspring) with trailer, filmographies, weblinks and excerpt from Jacques Demy documentary. VHS (Electric Pictures), deleted.

Now Try These: Aimée previously starred in *Les Mauvaises Rencontres* (1955), the debut of critic Alexandre Astruc, who wrote of the influential camera-as-pen theory. She reprised the role of Lola in Demy's American feature *The Model Shop* (1969).

For his first feature film, François Truffaut had considered an adaptation of Henri-Pierre Roché's historical romance, *Jules et Jim*. Roché's novel was published in 1953 and the director had read it soon after its publication. He met up with Roché but eventually decided that the task of adapting the novel would probably be too difficult for his first film. The project was sidelined while he made *Les Quatre Cents Coups*.

Then, after completing his David Goodis adaptation, *Tirez Sur le Pianiste*, Truffaut set about bringing Roché's novel to the screen, casting Jeanne Moreau in the lead role. Moreau and Truffaut began to shoot their version of Roché's book in April 1961. Despite the novel's additional settings of Germany and Greece, filming took place entirely in France. Unlike his adaptation of Goodis' *Down There*, *Jules et Jim* is remarkably faithful to its source material.

Jules et Jim (1961)

Alternative Title: *Jules and Jim*

Cast: Jeanne Moreau (Catherine), Oskar Werner (Jules), Henri Serre (Jim), Vanna Urbino (Gilberte), Boris Bassiak (Albert), Sabine Haudepin (Sabine), Marie Dubois (Thérèse), Danielle Bassiak (Albert's friend).

Crew: Directed by François Truffaut. Written by Jean Gruault and François Truffaut. Adapted from the novel *Jules et Jim* by Henri-Pierre Roché. Produced by Marcel Berbert. Cinematography by Raoul Coutard. Music by Georges Delerue. Words and music for 'Le Tourbillon' by Bassiak. 101 mins.

Story: Paris, 1912. Jules, a German-Austrian in Paris, befriends the Frenchman, Jim. At the house of mutual acquaintance, Albert, they see a slide of a sculpture that entrances them and leads them to decide that if they ever see a woman with the same smile, they will follow her. Sure enough, a short while later the two men meet a woman, Catherine, with the exact same smile. Jules begins a relationship with her and the three become inseparable. Jules and Catherine agree to marry but war breaks out, threatening to destroy the blissful triangle. During the war, Jules and Jim fear for each other's safety and contemplate the horror of killing the other in combat. Meanwhile, Catherine gives birth to a baby girl, Sabine.

After the war, Jim visits Catherine and Jules and finds their marriage has problems. Jules confesses that he fears Catherine will leave him and that she has had other lovers during their relationship. Catherine herself confides that she misses her freedom. Albert has become close to Catherine and wants to marry her and look after Sabine. Jim admits to his own love for her. Jules, overhearing the incident, sees a possible – if unconventional – way of saving the relationship. He urges Jim to love Catherine and allows their affair to take place in his house. This set-up soon turns sour.

Background: An early 19th century costume drama, Truffaut's *Jules et Jim* would, at first glance, seem streets away from the youthful explosion of the New Wave and may seem to have more in common with the mainstream 'tradition de qualité' the director rebuked so virulently in his *Cahiers* criticism. Especially when you consider that the source material was a novel written by a septuagenarian. A closer look at the *ménage à trois* subject matter, and an analysis of the film's lively visual style, and *Jules et Jim*'s status as a classic of the Nouvelle Vague is quickly confirmed.

Truffaut's third feature offers a catalogue of the director's recurrent concerns. Here is his delight in the bond of friendship, his love for children, a searing account of the destructive nature of romance and much lively debate about the arts and life in general. There are the director's usual irreverent gags and in-jokes too. Roché's novel had an autobiographical strain and at one stage Jim writes a book based on his own experiences, in which the lead characters are called Jacques and Julienne.

Like Truffaut's earlier films, *Jules et Jim* is littered with incidental delights (such as Jim and Catherine's feet touching under the table when they first meet) and a sense of play (Catherine dressing up as Thomas, Jules and Jim's sporty pursuits, the three friends' search for treasures in the countryside). This exuberant, effervescent approach is established in the film's title sequence, which plays rather like a trailer, showcasing key scenes to come and introducing the main players as they appear on the screen.

The breathless *joie de vivre* of these opening minutes is a marvel to behold, pre-empting the symbolic essence of 'Le Tourbillon,' the song Albert has written for Catherine. The film's first shot finds Jules and Jim opening up a case of costumes and Truffaut himself draws endless surprises from a bottomless case of cinematic tricks. His stylistic verve is dazzling. Raoul Coutard's handheld camerawork is especially fluid and the scenes in which Jules, Jim and Catherine cycle in the countryside and ramble through the fields reveal, in particular, the liberating quality of their friendship. Most noticeable are the swirling shots that intelligently complement the story.

In-Jokes: The opening line of the film is taken from Roché's second and only other novel, *Les Deux Anglaises et le Continent*, which Truffaut would also film in 1971. Cabaret artist Boris Bassiak appears in the film as Albert the musician. The song Albert has written for Catherine in the film was written by Bassiak himself.

The Verdict: At its premiere, *Jules et Jim* was given a 15-minute standing ovation. It remains arguably Truffaut's best-loved film and alongside *A Bout de Souffle* is probably the most often associated with the New Wave. Marie Dubois' puffer train impression, Catherine's jump into the river and Jules, Jim and Catherine's race across the bridge are all iconic moments from the movement. 5/5

Availability: VHS (Tartan) and Region 2 DVD (Tartan) including an audio commentary from Jeanne Moreau and reminiscences from Truffaut among other extras.

Now Try These: Paul Mazursky's *Willie and Phil* riffs on the film's central premise. For his directorial debut, *Keeping the Faith*, Edward Norton paid homage to *Jules et Jim*. Watch for the scene where Jenna Elfman is viewed from different perspectives in quick succession. Truffaut cast Werner again in his 1966 adaptation of Ray Bradbury's sci-fi novel *Fahrenheit 451*.

And Godard Created Karina, then Recreated Bardot

It's strange to imagine now, but Godard originally offered the role of *A Bout de Souffle*'s Patricia Franchini to Danish-born actress and former model Anna Karina. The director went on to cast the beautiful Karina in his second film, *Le Petit Soldat*, which was banned and then proved box-office poison. He immediately worked with her again in the kooky musical comedy *Une Femme est Une Femme*, which won Karina the Best Actress award at the 1961 Berlin Film Festival, where the picture also picked up the Special Jury Prize. Godard was to marry Karina that same year and she appears in several of his finest 60s films, including *Alphaville* and *Pierrot le Fou*.

In a 1962 interview with *Cahiers*, Godard explained that the inspiration for *Une Femme est Une Femme* came from a quote from Chaplin: "Tragedy is life in close-up, and comedy, life in long shot." Godard decided, "I'm going to make a comedy in close-up: the film will be tragic-comic." Alongside Karina, Godard cast Jean-Claude Brialy, who had already shown a flair for comedy with his performance in *Les Cousins*.

Une Femme est Une Femme (1961)

Alternative Title: *A Woman is a Woman*

Cast: Anna Karina (Angela), Jean-Claude Brialy (Emile Récamier), Jean-Paul Belmondo (Alfred Lubitsch), Marie Dubois (Angela's friend), Ernest Menzer (Bar Owner).

Crew: Directed and written by Jean-Luc Godard. Produced by Carlo Ponti and Georges de Beauregard. Cinematography by Raoul Coutard. Music by Michel Legrand. 80 mins.

Story: Angela wants a baby but her boyfriend Emile doesn't. Que faire? We follow Angela from her flat to the club where she works as a stripper and then back to the flat again. En route she meets friends for drinks, dips in and out of shops and quarrels with Emile. Her cry is always the same: "Je veux un enfant!" The answer to the problem eventually presents itself in the form of mutual friend Alfred, who believes himself the right man for the job.

Background: Godard's third film shares immediate similarities with his first. Reappearing from *A Bout de Souffle* are actor Jean-Paul Belmondo, cinematographer Raoul Coutard and the city of Paris itself. Both of these features have incredibly simple plots which are used as scaffolding for lovers' domestic digressions and lengthy debates. Both films are also affectionate pastiches of an established American genre. While *A Bout de Souffle* tipped its hat to the B-movie, this film hails the Hollywood musical. Later, Godard would riff on other established genres, such as the war film (*Les Carabiniers*), science fiction (*Alphaville*) and the crime caper (*Bande à Part*).

Karina's presence injects *Une Femme est Une Femme* with its unique charm. Like the rest of the cast, she is clearly having a ball. The actress brings buoyancy to the role of Angela and in many ways her character *is* the film – playful, stylish, sweet and sexy. Her performance is also as self-conscious as the movie itself. From the film's opening cry of "Lights! Camera! Action!", the audience's attention is repeatedly drawn to the fact that this is a movie. In one scene, Angela and Emile address the viewer from their kitchen and Angela announces, "Before acting out our little farce we should bow to the audience." In the opening and closing minutes, Angela also winks at the camera, showing us that she is in on the joke. Viewers might flash back, here, to Michel Poiccard addressing the audience from his stolen car in the first minutes of *A Bout de Souffle*.

In fact, this film often resembles a rehearsal for a film. Stage directions such as "Exit Angela" are given by the characters and there are frequent costume changes. These scenes also have a loose, improvised quality. In this manner, Godard resurrects the spirit of the back-stage musicals of the Great Depression, like Mervyn LeRoy's *Golddiggers of 1933* and Lloyd Bacon's *42nd Street*. Such films showed the events involved behind the scenes of an often-troubled production, combining dramatic incident with showy musical routines. As Demy did in *Lola*, Godard debases the traditional glitz and glamour of the musical. Angela works in the Zodiac, a tame, run-down and rather lacklustre strip joint distinctly lacking in razzmatazz. She performs her sailor-girl routine to a paltry smattering of observers. We're a world away here from the musicals of Cyd Charisse, Gene Kelly and Bob Fosse, with whom Angela longs to work.

Une Femme est Une Femme is a truly insouciant and effervescent work, bubbling with so many original ideas that you're constantly left playing catch up. If you blink, you're bound to miss something. Conversations, especially arguments, are punctuated with orchestral flourishes. Characters periodically burst into song and/or dance routines. At home, Emile picks up a brush, strums it like a guitar and serenades Angela. Seconds later, the brush is used as a piece of sporting equipment. Another highlight is the scene where an exasperated Angela and Emile exchange insults using words from the titles on book covers. Elsewhere, Angela challenges Alfred to mimic her every move, resulting in a funny run of stills with the pair assuming identical positions.

In-Jokes: The face of Catherine Demongeot (Zazie) can be seen on a magazine in the newsagents. Belmondo comments that he wants to go home so he can watch *A Bout de Souffle* on TV. Later on in a bar he asks Jeanne Moreau, "How goes it with Jules and Jim?" (The love triangle plot of that film is of course also echoed here.) Angela's friend is reading *Shoot the Piano Player*. The character is played by Marie Dubois, who starred in Truffaut's film. The surname of Belmondo's character reveals one of Godard's chief influences for the picture, American musical maestro Ernst Lubitsch. Emile and Angela's apartment actually belonged to Godard and Karina.

The Verdict: Towards the end of the film, Brialy's character comments, "I'm not sure if it's comedy or tragedy… But it's a masterpiece." He's not far wrong. *Une Femme est Une Femme* might be one of Godard's easiest films and it's also one of his most enjoyable. A delight to watch. 5/5

Availability: Included alongside *Le Petit Soldat* and *Alphaville* on Warner's three-disc Jean-Luc Godard DVD Collection (Region 2). VHS (Warner), deleted.

Now Try This: Jacques Demy made his own MGM-inspired musical, *Les Parapluies de Cherbourg*, in 1964.

In March and April of 1962, one year after the success of *Une Femme est Une Femme* at Berlin, Godard spent four weeks shooting another picture with Karina. *Vivre sa Vie* was to prove yet another departure for the director, who here employed a sort of Brechtian stylisation. It was also a change of pace for his lead actress, who swapped her cheeky, carefree style for a more reserved, sombre role. The film brought another festival success, winning a brace of awards at Venice.

Vivre sa Vie (1962)

Alternative Titles: *It's My Life, My Life to Live*

Cast: Anna Karina (Nana Kleinfrankenheim), Sady Rebbot (Raoul), André S Labarthe (Paul), Guylaine Schlumberger (Yvette), Gérard Hoffman (Le Chef), Monique Messine (Elisabeth), Paul Pavel (Journaliste).

Crew: Directed by Jean-Luc Godard. Written by Jean-Luc Godard and Marcel Sacotte. Based on *Où en est la Prostitution* by Marcel Sacotte. Produced by Pierre Braunberger. Cinematography by Raoul Coutard. Music by Michel Legrand. 85 mins.

Story: "Lend yourself to others and give yourself to yourself," is the advice offered by the French philosopher Montaigne at the start of this film. Nana is a penniless aspiring actress who works in a record store and is forced to lend, or rather sell, herself to others as a prostitute in Paris. She slowly learns more about the world's oldest profession and meets a series of clients in a run-down hotel. But when Nana is eventually taken by a pimp, she finds her destiny is out of her hands.

Background: The Karina of *Une Femme est Une Femme* is virtually unrecognisable in the opening minutes of *Vivre sa Vie*. A comparison of the films' prologues highlights their dramatic differences. In *Une Femme est Une Femme*, Karina flits along the streets, her mood as colourful as her outfit. In the title sequence of *Vivre sa Vie*, she wears understated clothes and is shot in a steely black and white from a variety of angles. The first proper scene is similarly detached and impersonal, as Karina's face is seen only in the reflection of a mirror behind the bar at which she's sitting.

The structure of these two films also couldn't be more different. Godard swaps the free flowing form of his musical for an episodic plan, as *Vivre sa Vie* is told in a series of 12 Brechtian tableaux, each introducing the key events of that section. This is a highly stylised, schematic exercise but, as the film progresses, there are more humorous and irreverent episodes that recall *Une Femme est Une Femme* and foreshadow Godard's later crime caper *Bande à Part*. These include a humorous scene where a man explodes an imaginary balloon and the episode in which Karina dances to a tune on the jukebox.

Ambitiously, the film attempts to blend B-movie elements into its narrative, as well as adopting a pseudo-documentary style comparable to Alain Resnais' *Hiroshima Mon Amour*. *Vivre sa Vie* works as a fictional story as well as a social record on prostitution in the 1960s. Facts and figures are steadily offered to the audience, from laws, decrees and various medical regulations of prostitution to fees and codes of behaviour. In an extraordinary sequence, Nana asks questions about prostitution which are answered by the narrator over a montage of her encounters with various clients. In this manner, the film foreshadows Godard's later experiments with the documentary form, most notably in *Deux ou Trois Choses Que Je Sais D'Elle*, in which he examined the same themes.

In-Jokes: A line from Max Ophüls' *Lola Montès* is quoted in the film. One of the posters in the background is for Otto Preminger's *Exodus*. A parallel is drawn between Karina and Renée Jeanne Falconetti, the actress in Carl Dreyer's *La Passion de Jeanne D'Arc*, which Nana watches with tears in her eyes. Towards the film's climax, the camera passes a cinema screening *Jules et Jim*. Anna Karina's character says she acted in a movie with Eddie Constantine. Two years later she would be starring opposite Constantine in Godard's *Alphaville*.

The Verdict: Godard novices should perhaps look elsewhere for a more digestible introduction to the director's work. Although the mix of tones and genres never quite comes off, *Vivre sa Vie* is an arresting and original feature that's full of ideas. Watch out for the staccato editing of a tracking shot inside a bar as gunfire sounds outside. 4/5

Availability: VHS (Nouveau Pictures) and Region 2 DVD (Nouveau Pictures) with gallery and booklet.

Now Try This: *Belle de Jour* (1967) is a surreal and satirical portrait of upmarket Parisian brothels, starring Catherine Deneuve and directed by Luis Buñuel.

With *Le Petit Soldat*, *Une Femme est Une Femme* and *Vivre sa Vie* in particular, Godard made a new star out of Karina. After *Vivre sa Vie*, he set about reinventing one of the very first actresses to be associated with the New Wave, Brigitte Bardot. She had frolicked semi-nude in Vadim's *Et Dieu Créa la Femme* and, aside from a stunning performance as a murdering femme fatale in Clouzot's *La Vérité* (1960), had often appeared as little more than unclothed eye candy in a string of disappointing features. With *Le Mépris*, Godard gave the actress her perfect role.

Le Mépris (1963)

Alternative Title: *Contempt*

Cast: Brigitte Bardot (Camille Javal), Jack Palance (Jeremy Prokosh), Michel Piccoli (Paul Javal), Georgia Moll (Francesca Vanini), Fritz Lang (Himself), Jean-Luc Godard (Assistant Director), Linda Véras (Siren), Raoul Coutard (Cameraman).

Crew: Directed and written by Jean-Luc Godard. Based on the novel *Il Disprezzo* by Alberto Moravia. Produced by Georges de Beauregard and Carlo Ponti. Cinematography by Raoul Coutard. Music by Georges Delerue. 100 mins.

Story: A man and a beautiful naked woman are alone in a bedroom. Slowly, the woman asks the man which bits of her body he finds the most attractive. Understandably, he cannot decide, but nevertheless professes total love for her. This opening scene is almost unbearably sexy. The man, Paul Javal, is a talented young author with a number of detective novels under his belt. The woman, Camille, is his wife. When Paul is offered a screenwriting job adapting scenes from *The Odyssey* he accepts, in order to work with the acclaimed German director Fritz Lang. As the shoot progresses, however, Paul loses faith in the movie and its American producer, Jerry Prokosh. Meanwhile, Camille gradually develops an overwhelming contempt for her husband. The couple travel to Capri to stay in Prokosh's villa while certain scenes are shot. During this time their relationship disintegrates in the heat.

Background: Godard described *Le Mépris* as a simple film about complicated ideas. Famous for its montage sequences and long takes (there are only 149 of them in the whole film), this is an impressively faithful adaptation of Italian author Alberto Moravia's analytical novel *Il Disprezzo*. The story of a writer who lives in Rome and struggles with feelings of 'selling out' when working on the movie in Capri, it is clearly autobiographical to a certain extent. Moravia was born in Rome and wrote for the screen as well as penning a series of acclaimed novels, short stories and selected non-fiction.

Moravia's *Il Disprezzo* is written in the first person by the character of the husband who 'sets out to relate how, while I continued to love her and not to judge her, Emilia [Camille in the film], on the other hand, discovered, or thought she discovered, certain defects in me, and judged me and in consequence ceased to love me.' Godard maintains the painfully slow, measured pace of the novel in his film, although he loses the husband's intensely personal and anguished voice, as he sifts through the past to try to understand how his relationship with his wife fell apart. In the novel the character almost takes on the role of an investigator in his proceedings, searching for evidence in his wife's behaviour. In Godard's film, both the husband and the wife have intermittent voice-overs, and this increases the range of the examination of their marriage.

With another key change, Godard makes the producer American (in the novel he is Italian). This means that three of the lead characters have different nationalities, which calls for a translator. Their laboriously translated conversations reaffirm the communication breakdown theme. The producer can't see the writer's point of view or the director's, the husband can't understand the behaviour of his wife, which she herself – perhaps – also cannot fathom. In an important scene, Lang, Jerry and Paul attempt, with great difficulty, to hold a conversation with the aid of the translator over the noise of a musical performance. Of course, making the producer American also allows Godard to make cracks at American production and Jerry is often referred to derisively as, "that American." Mirroring the on screen action, Godard himself argued with the producers of *Le Mépris*, who wanted to make the film more commercial and have Bardot wear less clothing. The opening scene is a concession to their demands.

In-Jokes: *Le Mépris* is littered with them. The famous opening scene recalls one of Patricia and Michel's conversations in *A Bout de Souffle* and a proclamation of love from Emile in *Une Femme est Une Femme*. Posters can be seen in the background for Hitchcock's *Psycho* and Godard's own *Vivre sa Vie*. Just as Michel Poiccard dressed like Bogart in *A Bout de Souffle*, Paul Javal tries to emulate Dean Martin in Vincente Minnelli's *Some Came Running*. (He also dresses like an American PI, which is appropriate enough for his investigations into his wife's behaviour.) Godard portrays an assistant director. For the part of the German auteur-director (called Rheingold in the original novel), Godard cast Fritz Lang to play himself. Ironically, in the novel, the narrator comments that Rheingold is 'not in the same class as the Pabsts and Langs.' Discussions on Lang's *M* and *Rancho Notorious* are included. Interestingly, Godard also considered Carl Dreyer (whose *La Passion de Jeanne D'Arc* plays in *Vivre sa Vie*) for the part.

The Verdict: As the trailer claimed, this is indeed "a tragic love story in a fabulous setting" and a "fabulous love story in a tragic setting." Exquisite, erotic and erudite. 5/5

Availability: VHS (Connoisseur Video) and Region 2 DVD (Momentum) with a featurette on Godard and Bardot, and Jacques Rozier's short film *Paparazzi*, concerning the incredible press reaction to Bardot.

Now Try These: As a film about film-making, *Le Mépris* rivals Wilder's *Sunset Boulevard*, Minnelli's *The Bad and the Beautiful* and Truffaut's *La Nuit Américaine*. Martin Scorsese reused George Delerue's Baroque score for *Le Mépris* in his own multiple voice-over epic *Casino*.

For his next collaboration with Karina, Godard chose to film another irreverent, pulpy crime thriller on the streets of Paris. Nominally based on a novel called *Fool's Gold*, *Bande à Part* was shot on a tight schedule (less than four weeks). The film was the first production of Godard and Karina's new company, Anouchka, which was also the director's nickname for his star.

Bande à Part (1964)

Alternative Titles: *Band of Outsiders, The Outsiders*

Cast: Anna Karina (Odile), Sami Frey (Franz), Claude Brasseur (Arthur), Louisa Colpeyne (Aunt), Danièle Girard (English teacher).

Crew: Directed and written by Jean-Luc Godard. Based on the novel *Fool's Gold* by Dolores and Bert Hitchens. Cinematography by Raoul Coutard. Music by Michel Legrand. 95 mins.

Story: Two petty crooks cruise the streets of Paris. Arthur is a Charles Aznavour lookalike, Franz a self-styled gangster straight out of a Cagney movie. Before they have shared more than a few words, they spot Odile, a young woman who Franz has grown close to over the previous two weeks. They drive on through the suburbs and reach the house where Odile lives with her Aunt Victoria. Her aunt's friend, Mr Stolz, has apparently amassed quite a fortune in cash here. Having cased the joint, the two crooks attend an English lesson back in town, where they meet up with Odile.

After class, Arthur and Franz quiz Odile about Stolz's money. She finds herself bullied into taking part in a heist at her aunt's house. The following morning, Arthur's suspicious uncle makes Arthur promise to undertake the heist without Franz or Odile. Arthur placates them, but then swiftly brings the date for the job forward and tells the others it must happen that night...

Background: File *Bande à Part* alongside Truffaut's *Tirez Sur le Pianiste*. The lyrical, pulpy imagery of Godard's film is particularly reminiscent of Goodis' novels. Both films are highly unconventional takes on the crime genre with 'outsiders' in the lead roles and an interest more in digressions, incidental occurrences and gestures than the grand machinations of plot. Still, *Bande à Part* has a quintessential genre scenario (the big heist) and is brimful of crime iconography. Franz, played by Sami Frey, has the angular face of a Warner's criminal and is also dressed for the part, with his cocked hat, double-breasted oversized jacket and raincoat. He leaves a film noir shadow wherever he goes. Like Michel Poiccard, Franz is playing the role of the gangster, informed from his love for American thrillers.

Similarly, Godard's direction has been influenced by the film noir style. As well as the chiaroscuro lighting effects and edgy close-ups of characters' faces (including, at one point, even the face on Stolz's hidden banknotes), much of the framing comes straight out of American B-movies. A notable example is the recurrent midshot of Franz and Arthur, as seen from behind, in their car.

There are many parallels to other New Wave films. Truffaut's *Jules et Jim* and Godard's own *Une Femme est*

Une Femme are evoked by the central love triangle. *Bande à Part* also shares *Une Femme est Une Femme*'s sense of play, particularly in the musical sequence. Several quirky comic touches, such as the antics of the liquor-swigging older student in the English class and the central trio's record-breaking sprint around the Louvre (9 minutes, 43 seconds to be exact), also recall the irreverence of *Une Femme est Une Femme* and *Tirez Sur le Pianiste*. The famous 'minute's silence' sequence (which harks back to a moment in the director's early short *Une Histoire d'Eau*) could be straight out of either film.

Godard gleefully speeds up sequences in *Bande à Part* and much of the humour relies on physical comedy, such as Franz and Arthur's exaggerated bad-guy swagger and the stylised shoot-out scenes (directly influenced by Melville's *Bob le Flambeur*). The film is famous for the stylish set piece in which the three leads share a dance routine, the Madison, in a café. Godard stops the music intermittently to give us an insight into what the characters are thinking during the scene, echoing *Une Femme est Une Femme*, where characters' thoughts are explained through intertitles.

In-Jokes: Too many to mention here! In the credits, the director appears as Jean-Luc Cinéma Godard, and as usual this film reveals a typically Godardian cinematic self-consciousness. After five minutes the narrator (Godard himself) offers "a clue for latecomers" and sums up the plot so far. Towards the film's close he tells us "My story ends here like a dime novel." Aunt Victoria's comment to Odile ("I hope you go to class

and not to the movies") is surely a reference to
Godard's student days. The characters in the film drive
past a store with a neon sign proclaiming 'nouvelle
vague.' Odile recreates a scene from Charlie Chaplin's
The Gold Rush and the film's final scene pays homage
to Chaplin's *The Immigrant*. You'll also find a reference
to *La Peau Douce*.

The Verdict: There's so much to savour in this fresh,
funny and effortlessly likeable film, not least the strong
performances of the leads, especially the ever-impres-
sive Karina. The title sequence itself is a work of art.
Cool, witty and utterly irresistible. 5/5

Availability: VHS (BFI) and Region 2 DVD (BFI)
with a wealth of extras including interviews with
Coutard and Karina, an A–Z guide and other goodies.

Now Try These: The dance scene influenced Uma
Thurman and John Travolta's boogie in Tarantino's *Pulp
Fiction* and is also echoed in Hal Hartley's *Simple Men*.
The characters in Bernardo Bertolucci's *The Dreamers*
race through the Louvre and beat the record set by
Odile, Franz and Arthur.

Songs, Thrills and a Town
Called Alphaville

In 1963, having filmed a short, second instalment of the
Antoine Doinel story (*Antoine et Colette*) and while
working on his 'Hitchbook' (a lengthy study of Alfred
Hitchcock), François Truffaut intended to film an adaptation of Ray Bradbury's sci-fi novel *Fahrenheit 451*.
However, he was forced to postpone the project and
proceeded to film *La Peau Douce* instead. This often-
overlooked follow-up to *Jules et Jim* also deals with a
love triangle, albeit a rather more conventional one, in
which a married man conducts an affair with another
woman. Fittingly, considering Truffaut's parallel
research on the work of Hitch, *La Peau Douce* is an edgy
endeavour which maintains a high level of tension
throughout. It marks the beginning of a series of
Truffaut thrillers including *La Mariée Etait en Noir* and
La Sirène du Mississippi.

La Peau Douce (1964)

Alternative Titles: *Silken Skin*, *The Soft Skin*

Cast: Jean Desailly (Pierre Lachenay), Françoise
Dorléac (Nicole), Nelly Benedetti (Franca), Daniel

Caccaldi (Clément), Laurence Badie (Ingrid), Sabine Haudepin (Sabine), Philippe Dumat (Reims Cinéma Manager).

Crew: Directed by François Truffaut. Written by Jean-Louis Richard and François Truffaut. Produced by Antonio Da Cunha Telles. Cinematography by Raoul Coutard. Music by Georges Delerue. 113 mins.

Story: Pierre Lachenay is an author, intellectual and minor celebrity who lives in Paris with his wife. Travelling to Lisbon, where he is to give a talk on Balzac, he falls for an attractive airline stewardess named Nicole. When he later encounters the younger woman in his hotel, he asks her to join him for a drink. They get on extremely well and eventually return to Nicole's room to consummate their new relationship. The following day, Lachenay returns to Paris.

Back at home, the writer cannot stop thinking about Nicole and arranges to meet up with her. After a series of brief encounters, they grow frustrated at the lack of time they are able to spend together. In order to guarantee a definite period of intimacy, Lachenay agrees to give a talk in Reims and the couple escape for a few days. But it's only a matter of time before their indiscretions catch up with them.

Background: Ever since Antoine Doinel spotted his mother sharing an illicit embrace on the streets of Paris in *Les Quatre Cents Coups*, adultery was to prove a key theme in Truffaut's oeuvre. The director often remarked that the germ of *La Peau Douce* was the image of a couple in the back seat of a taxi locked in a passionate kiss, their teeth knocking. As its title suggests, *La Peau Douce* is one of Truffaut's most sensuous films. The opening sequence shows two pairs of interlocking hands and, throughout the film, the director frequently employs close-ups of different parts of the body. When Lachenay and Nicole share their first night together, we see her hand turn on the light in the room and his quickly turn it off. Then, in semi-darkness, the couple touch each other's faces. Returning home, Lachenay is met at the airport by his wife and we see their hands placed over each other's on opposite sides of the glass in the arrival lounge. In another striking scene, Lachenay watches Nicole change her shoes from behind a curtain, recalling the way Catherine changes clothes behind a screen in *Jules et Jim*.

Truffaut worried that *La Peau Douce* would become an unsavoury film, with an unsympathetic lead character. For the main role, he originally wanted François Périer, star of Federico Fellini's *Le Notti di Cabiria*. The part of Lachenay would, instead, be marvellously played by a sad-eyed, slightly crumpled-looking Jean Desailly, who had recently appeared with Jean-Paul Belmondo in Jean-Pierre Melville's *Le Doulos*. Desailly brings to the role a certain sense of compulsion and middle-aged helplessness, as well as the sense of a desperate man clinging to a new lease of life. Perhaps best known as Catherine Deneuve's older sister, Françoise Dorléac is stunning as the young stewardess. The actress, who had also recently starred with Belmondo (in *L'Homme de Rio*), was to die tragically in an automobile accident on the way to Nice airport at the age of 25, just four years after making *La Peau Douce*.

As a thriller, *La Peau Douce* rivals *Ascenseur Pour L'Echafaud*. The films share a number of similarities, not just in subject matter. The final truth is given away in both by conclusive photographic evidence, which is perhaps one of the few weaknesses in Truffaut's film. This predictable plotline aside, *La Peau Douce* delivers some real surprises. Its chilling and melodramatic ending (amazingly inspired by a newspaper report of a real-life incident) leaves the viewer reeling.

A note of trivia: During their stay at the chalet in the countryside, Nicole places a breakfast tray outside their room. A cat swiftly arrives and sniffs around the tray. The difficulties involved in setting up such a shot are displayed in an almost identical scene in Truffaut's film about film-making, *La Nuit Américaine*.

In-Jokes: The apartment in the film was Truffaut's own. Lachenay was the surname of Truffaut's best friend from childhood. Truffaut wrote some of his film criticism using the same surname.

The Verdict: Like *Tirez Sur le Pianiste*, *La Peau Douce* flopped on its initial release but has since gained a considerable amount of critical acclaim. The assured ensemble acting, moving score and well-judged pace combine to make it one of the more unsung classics of the New Wave. 4/5

Availability: Region 2 DVD (Tartan) includes an insightful commentary from screenwriter Jean-Louis

Richard, a featurette on Françoise Dorléac and a discussion on selected scenes from Truffaut. VHS (Artificial Eye), deleted.

Now Try This: Truffaut's *La Femme D'A Côté* (1981) is another film about adultery, again scored by Georges Delerue.

While her sister embraced the world of the thriller with *La Peau Douce*, Catherine Deneuve busied herself with one of the most ambitious and popular musicals of the period, Jacque Demy's *Les Parapluies de Cherbourg*. This unique endeavour was Demy's third feature. After *Lola*, he had directed an episode of the 1962 omnibus film *Les Sept Péchés Capitaux* (other contributors included Claude Chabrol, Jean-Luc Godard and Roger Vadim) and a second feature, *La Baie des Anges*.

Les Parapluies de Cherbourg (1964)

Alternative Title: *The Umbrellas of Cherbourg*

Cast: Catherine Deneuve (Geneviève Emery), Nino Castelnuovo (Guy), Anne Vernon (Madame Emery), Marc Michel (Roland Cassard), Ellen Farner (Madeleine), Mireille Perrey (Aunt Elise).

Crew: Directed and written by Jacques Demy. Produced by Mag Bodard. Cinematography by Jean Rabier. Music by Michel Legrand. 91 mins.

Story: November 1957. Geneviève, a 17-year-old,

works in an umbrella shop run by her mother, in the town of Cherbourg. Her beau, Guy, works as a mechanic in a nearby garage. Guy and Geneviève plan to marry, buy a filling station and live happily ever after, but their dream is frowned upon by Geneviève's mother, who disapproves of the mechanic and thinks her daughter is too young to get married anyway. She considers diamond-seller Roland a far more suitable suitor. When Guy leaves Cherbourg for Algeria, to carry out his military service, Geneviève is heartbroken. Her position is further compromised when she finds herself pregnant two months after his departure.

Background: From the plot description, *Les Parapluies de Cherbourg* sounds like a heavy slice of social realism or a trivial straight-to-video saga. In the capable hands of Jacques Demy, however, it is a tender, nostalgic and elegant romance in which all the characters sing their lines – each and every last one – and the streets are painted in a range of beautiful colour-coded pastel shades. Demy's original idea, to film *Lola* as a grandiose colourful musical, had been compromised by his modest budget. You'll notice that the only song-and-dance numbers in that film are off-the-cuff rehearsals in the studio, rather than show-stopping routines. Having been forced to shoot in black and white on that occasion, there is therefore a sense of triumph in the opening minutes of *Les Parapluies de Cherbourg*, where colour is splashed across every inch of the screen.

The film opens with an iris, an old-fashioned technique that Demy often used to introduce or end his films. An aerial view then shows rain-soaked cobbled streets, across which the towns-people of Cherbourg pass, many hidden beneath umbrellas. We sweep through the lives of the main characters and, impressively, Demy manages to maintain the tempo of the film's opening number for the entire running time. His film grows beyond gimmicky concept to become a sort of pop opera. The 20-year-old Deneuve gives an assured performance, as do the supporting players, but the real stars are arguably Michel Legrand's score and Jean Rabier's cinematography.

In-Jokes: "People only die of love in films," comments Geneviève's mother. There's a photo of Marilyn Monroe pinned up in the mechanics' quarters. Marc Michel's character has the same name as his character in *Lola*.

The Verdict: This exquisite New Wave fairy tale overshadowed *La Peau Douce* when it was screened at Cannes. It won Demy the coveted Palme d'Or and also picked up five Oscar® nominations, not to mention the Prix Louis Delluc. Its popularity with critics and film lovers hasn't waned in the years since. There's really no other film quite like *Les Parapluies de Cherbourg*. You could frame each and every scene. 4/5

Availability: VHS (Tartan) and Region 2 DVD (Tartan) with film notes, biographies and a photo gallery.

Now Try This: Deneuve went on to star alongside Dorléac in Demy's next feature, *Les Demoiselles de Rochefort*.

In 1962, Godard turned his attention to science fiction with his intriguing Italian-language short *Il Nuovo Mondo* (*The New World*). The 20-minute film was made as part of the *RoGoPaG* anthology, which also featured contributions from Pasolini, Rossellini and Gregoretti. Godard wasn't the only New Wave director to show an interest in science fiction. Chris Marker's *La Jetée* also displays an influence and Truffaut's first colour film, *Fahrenheit 451*, was an adaptation of a fantasy written by Ray Bradbury.

For Godard, *Il Nuovo Mondo* pointed the way to a full-length film, *Alphaville*, which was shot in just two weeks at the end of 1965. This dystopian vision proved a typically Godardian blend of genres – a hard-boiled sci-fi flick with elements from comic books and pop art. The film won Godard the Golden Bear at the 1965 Berlin Film Festival and remains one of his most popular works. It seems to constantly play in repertory cinemas and in 2000 was screened at London's IMAX cinema, with an atmospheric live musical accompaniment from Scanner.

Alphaville (1965)

Alternative Title: *Alphaville: Une Etrange Aventure de Lemmy Caution*

Cast: Eddie Constantine (Lemmy Caution), Anna Karina (Natacha Von Braun), Akim Tamiroff (Henri Dickson), Howard Vernon (Professor Von Braun), Laszlo Szabo (Chief Engineer), Michel Delahaye (Von Braun's Assistant).

Crew: Directed and written by Jean-Luc Godard. Based on the novel *La Capitale de la Douleur* by Paul Eluard. Produced by André Michelin. Cinematography by Raoul Coutard. Music by Paul Misraki. 95 mins.

Story: Lemmy Caution, a stone-faced secret agent from the Outland, arrives at a hotel in Alphaville and checks in under the guise of Ivan Johnson, newspaper reporter. Each of this hotel's rooms comes with its own jukebox, bible and sinisterly seductive bathing assistant. The PI is in town on a deadly mission: to put an end to the rule of a giant, emotionless computer called Alpha 60 that runs the city of Alphaville, where love is illegal. In Alphaville, people who behave illogically are assassinated and no one understands the meaning of 'conscience'. To succeed, Caution must find and "bring back or liquidate" the mysterious Professor Von Braun, the brains behind the machine. When Caution meets the professor's beautiful daughter, Natacha, he is determined to save her from this cold world and escort her safely to the Outland.

Background: Perhaps Godard's greatest achievement in *Alphaville* is the creation of the hermetic, high-security city of Alphaville itself. Characteristically, Godard eschewed building the expensive, expansive sets, typically favoured by sci-fi directors, and instead shot the film on the streets of Paris. Some great Parisian locations were handpicked and then injected with a futuristic sheen, as in *Il Nuovo Mondo*, thanks to Raoul Coutard's steely black and white cinematography. You can still visit the place where Caution stays. It's the Scribe Hotel near the Place de l'Opéra.

113

Dark, impersonal and neon-lit, the city itself becomes a character in the film, more foreboding and perhaps more threatening than even the enigmatic Professor himself. At the centre of *Alphaville* is the iconic Constantine, who Godard likened to a "solid block" in the film. Constantine appears in every scene here. With his heavy, wrinkled brow, haunted eyes and craggy, pockmarked face, he's quite a sight. Constantine's performance of unerring conviction holds *Alphaville* together. He plays Caution without so much as a knowing wink that he's assuming the kind of role that he made his own in a host of 1950s and 1960s detective films (including six as Lemmy Caution).

How does one describe *Alphaville* to someone who hasn't been there? The swimming pool killings, the hotel's different classes of seductresses, the belching bullfrog narration – this is a unique world. It's perhaps best not to concern yourself with the plot but instead savour the film's incidental delights, such as Caution sparking his cigarette lighter with a bullet from his pistol or bludgeoning an attacker to the sound of Paul Misraki's ironically beautiful music. There's some fine costume design too, from the standard-issue hats and macs for the boys to Karina's exquisite outfits and the seductresses' sexy dresses.

In-Jokes: References are made to Dick Tracy, Marcel Carné's *Le Jour se Lève* and Godard's own *A Bout de Souffle*. Caution quotes a line from *Hamlet* while Alpha 60 quotes from Jorge Luis Borges. Caution reads a copy of Raymond Chandler's *The Big Sleep*, a hard-boiled novel that also concerns a detective who is sucked into a plot involving an old man and his daughter. Jean-Pierre Léaud makes a blink-and-you'll-miss-it cameo.

The Verdict: A bizarre and beguiling slice of science fiction with an arresting visual design. The eerie atmospherics linger long after the film has finished. 4/5

Availability: Included on Warner's nattily-packaged, three-disc Jean-Luc Godard DVD Collection (Region 2) alongside *Le Petit Soldat* and *Une Femme est Une Femme*. VHS (Warner) is deleted.

Now Try This: In 1991 Godard and Constantine collaborated on another Lemmy Caution adventure, *Germany Year 90 Nine Zero*.

Before he made *Bande à Part*, Godard attempted to film an adaptation of *Obsession* by Lionel White, the author of the source material for Stanley Kubrick's taut crime pic *The Killing*. Godard wanted to cast Sylvie Vartan in the lead female role, but she refused so the project was subsequently put on hold. After he had completed *Bande à Part*, he envisaged making the film with Anna Karina and Richard Burton, but this also fell through. Later on, Belmondo came onboard and Godard decided that the film would tell the story of the "last romantic couple." The end result is a testament to the magnetic screen presence of both Belmondo and Karina.

Pierrot le Fou (1965)

Alternative Title: *Pierrot Goes Wild*

Cast: Jean-Paul Belmondo (Ferdinand Griffon, Pierrot), Anna Karina (Marianne), Dick Sanders (Fred), Graziella Galvani (Ferdinand's wife), Raymond Devos (Man on the pier), Aicha Abadir (Herself), Samuel Fuller (Himself).

Crew: Directed and written by Jean-Luc Godard. Based on the novel *Obsession* by Lionel White. Produced by Georges de Beauregard. Cinematography by Raoul Coutard. Music by Boris Bassiak and Antoine Duhamel. 110 mins.

Story: Ferdinand, the husband of a rich Italian woman, returns home from a dismal party. Bored, he offers a ride to his kids' babysitter, the attractive student Marianne. Before long, they decide to take a one-way street out of Paris and head for the South of France. Their impromptu journey will involve a bag of loot that goes up in flames, some gun-running shenanigans and auto theft as they resolve to hook up with Marianne's brother. The adventure sees them falling in love and ends with Ferdinand painting his face blue, wrapping dynamite to his head and lighting the fuse.

Background: As fast and loose a film as Godard has ever made, *Pierrot le Fou* recalls Howard Hawks' maxim, that a movie's plot could really be just an excuse for some good scenes. Here, Godard spins another girl-

and-gun, lovers-on-the-lam yarn in order to unfold a characteristically autonomous procession of digressions, stories, set pieces, references, satirical swipes, discursive debates, tongue-in-cheek gags and flights of fancy. One highlight is Karina's charming rendition of a song about her fate-line. The film abounds in ideas but some critics considered it a little too scattershot for its own good. In September 1965, *Variety*'s reviewer thought it "repetitive and precious rather than inventive and fresh" and recommended pruning to increase its commercial appeal.

The film provides a fitting end to this study of the French New Wave, as it represents a natural culmination, not only of the younger Godard's provocative film-making techniques, but also of the characteristics of the New Wave itself. Numerous comparisons to other films present themselves. Like *Jules et Jim*, it tells of an *amour fou* and features music from Bassiak. The exuberant musical interludes recall both *Les Parapluies de Cherbourg* and *Une Femme est Une Femme* while the colours (especially the use of filters), montage sequences and double narrative technique might remind us of *Le Mépris*. Like *Vivre sa Vie*, the film is told in short chapter-like instalments, this time introduced by brief phrases. The many references to writers, and the importance of Ferdinand's diary, highlight the New Wave's interest in literature. ("Life is so different from books," sighs Karina's character.)

Like *A Bout de Souffle*, the film divides its time between action sequences and pensive, discursive scenes. It serves up a typically Godardian buffet of both high and low culture references. Just as he had mixed

Faulkner with Bogart in his first film, here the director includes references to art, poetry, film and philosophy. Like TS Eliot's *The Waste Land*, the film is a kind of patchwork of references. The artists mentioned range from modern masters, like pop art maestro Roy Liechtenstein, to classical greats such as the 17th-century Spanish painter Velázquez. The writers who are referenced are similarly varied and include Honoré de Balzac, Robert Browning ("a poet named revolver"), Raymond Chandler, Joseph Conrad, F Scott Fitzgerald and William Shakespeare.

. Recalling Fritz Lang's appearance in *Le Mépris*, the influential American auteur Sam Fuller appears briefly as himself. Ferdinand meets him at a party where the director says he is in town to film *Les Fleurs du Mal*, apparently an adaptation of Baudelaire's collection of poems. Fuller declares that his film will be like a battle ground, encompassing love, hate, action and violence: "in one word, emotions." *Pierrot le Fou* can claim the same. This is a dazzling assault on the senses.

In-Jokes: As a tribute to Howard Hawks, Ferdinand calls Marianne "My Girl Friday." Near the opening we are told that Ferdinand's kids have been to the cinema for the third time that week. They have seen Nicholas Ray's *Johnny Guitar*, reminding us of Godard's belief that "Nicholas Ray IS cinema." Ferdinand and Marianne escape from a petrol station without paying, by using a Laurel and Hardy gag. One of the characters tells us he's being employed as a film extra. Searching for Marianne, Ferdinand enquires of a young girl: "Have you seen a young woman looking like a

Hollywood movie in Technicolor?" Ferdinand's declaration "Allons-y Alonso" was also used by Michel in *A Bout de Souffle*.

The Verdict: A film about liberty and reinvention, *Pierrot le Fou* is the product of a director at the height of his powers. There simply isn't another film quite like it. 5/5

Availability: Included with *Made in USA* and *Prénom Carmen* on Warner's three-disc Jean-Luc Godard DVD Collection: Volume 2 (Region 2). VHS (Electric Pictures), deleted.

Now Try These: *Pierrot le Fou*'s pop art commentary on advertising and consumerism echoes his *Une Femme Mariée* and looks forward to *La Chinoise*, *Masculin Féminin* and *Week-End*.

Further Viewing

It is nearly impossible to give a complete rundown of titles that are associated with the French New Wave, but this section offers a selection of works by the key directors of the movement.

L'Amour en Fuite (1979)

Alternative Title: *Love on the Run*

Directed by François Truffaut. Starring Jean-Pierre Léaud, Marie-France Pisier, Claude Jade. 94 mins.

Filmed nine years after its predecessor, *Domicile Conjugal*, the finale to Truffaut's Antoine Doinel cycle delivers none of the drama suggested by its title, but instead finds Antoine looking back on his life after his break-up with Christine (Claude Jade). Cue a patchwork of clips from the earlier films, which serves to stir nostalgia for the peerless *Les Quatre Cents Coups* and also emphasises the questionable necessity of a fifth episode in the story of Truffaut's cinematic alter-ego. Still, this scrapbook has a flurry of typically acute observations on relationships and Marie-France Pisier, one of the four contributors to the screenplay, is impressive as one of Antoine's former conquests. *The Verdict:* 3/5

Availability: Region 1 DVD (Fox Lorber) and part of Criterion's *The Adventures of Antoine Doinel* boxset. VHS (Artificial Eye), deleted.

L'Année Dernière à Marienbad (1961)

Alternative Title: *Last Year at Marienbad*

Directed by Alain Resnais. Starring Delphine Seyrig, Giorgio Albertazzi, Sascha Pitoëff. 94 mins.

Inspired by André Breton and Alfred Hitchcock, Alain Resnais conjured this deliciously elliptical puzzle of a movie. In a hotel, a man (X) and a woman (A) disagree over whether or not they have met before and X tries to get A to leave her husband, (M). Enigmatic study of time and memory or pretentious shaggy dog story? You will either love or hate this film, from one of the most intellectual of the New Wave directors. The plot is used as the framework for exceptionally stylish visual sequences, some intelligent editing and eye-catching photography. Whether X met A at Marienbad last year or not, there's certainly no questioning the feature's sheer originality. *The Verdict:* 4/5 *Availability:* Region 2 DVD (Optimum) with filmed introduction from critic Ginette Vincendeau. VHS (Connoisseur), deleted.

Antoine et Colette (1962)

Alternative Title: *Antoine and Colette*

Directed by François Truffaut. Starring Jean-Pierre Léaud, Marie-France Pisier, Patrick Auffay. 29 mins.

In Truffaut's short contribution to the five-part omnibus film *L'Amour à Vingt Ans*, Antoine Doinel has reached adolescence, moved out of his home and fallen in love with a girl called (you guessed it) Colette. He also has a job, with which he is making similarly slow progress. Written by Truffaut, cut by his regular editor Claudine Bouché and scored by another long-term collaborator, Georges Delerue, the film was photographed by the legendary Henri-Cartier Bresson. The other four shorts comprising *L'Amour à Vingt Ans* were directed by Andrzej Wajda, Shintaro Ishihara, Marcel Ophüls (son of Max '*Lola Montès*' Ophüls) and Renzo Rossellini (brother of Roberto). *The Verdict:* 3/5 *Availability:* Included on *Baisers Volés* VHS (Artificial Eye), deleted. Part of Criterion's *The Adventures of Antoine Doinel* boxset (Region 1 DVD) and on a Region 1 DVD with *Les Mistons* (Fox Lorber).

L'Argent de Poche (1976)

Alternative Titles: *Pocket Money, Small Change*

Directed by François Truffaut. Starring Geory Desmouceaux, Philippe Goldmann, Jean-François Stévenin. 101 mins.

Truffaut effectively bottled the essence of childhood with this colourful tale of the 'mistons' at a school in Thiers. Opening with an exuberant sequence, following a flood of children cascading down the town steps, the film flits from one scene to the next as if mimicking the short attention span of a young child. Made in some of the same spirit as Federico Fellini's

Amarcord, these assorted pick 'n' mix scenes convey the curiosity, sincerity, vulgarity and quick wit of the young, as well as the peculiarities of childish logic. Among the highlights are one boy's devotion to his disabled father and secret passion for a friend's mother, a practical guide to breastfeeding and the obligatory scene of two kids sneaking into a cinema. Bustling with the songs, rhymes and jokes of the playground, this is a funny-touching-tender work. Watch out for Truffaut's cameo in the opening minutes. *The Verdict:* 3/5 *Availability:* Region 2 DVD (MGM) with trailer.

Atlantic City (1980)

Alternative Title: *Atlantic City USA*

Directed by Louis Malle. Starring Burt Lancaster, Susan Sarandon, Michel Piccoli. 105 mins.

Famous for an opening scene that sees Susan Sarandon rubbing lemon juice into her body, *Atlantic City* is Louis Malle's finest English-language film. (The follow-up to 1978's *Pretty Baby*, it is one of a series of American features made by the director that includes the conversation piece *My Dinner with André* and Deep South drama *Alamo Bay*.) New in town, Sarandon is struggling to make a living and learning how to deal cards in a casino. Her neighbour, Lancaster, hasn't left Atlantic City for 20 years. A wistful, ageing conman, he runs a faltering numbers racket by day and watches Sarandon at night. When Sarandon's husband (who left her for her sister) comes to town to sell Mafia-owned coke, the two neighbours are brought together in an

unlikely relationship. A stunning ensemble achievement, the film has a script written by playwright John
Guare, music from Michel Legrand and a tour-de-force
performance from Lancaster as the character who – like
the town itself – can't stop himself from self-mytholo-
gising. *The Verdict:* 4/5 *Availability:* VHS (Arrow),
deleted. Region 1 DVD (Paramount).

La Baie des Anges (1962)

Alternative Titles: *Bay of Angels, Bay of the Angels*

Directed by Jacques Demy. Starring Jeanne Moreau,
Claude Mann, Paul Guers. 85 mins.

Inspired by a trip to a Cannes casino with Agnès
Varda, Demy's follow-up to *Lola* traces the downward
spiral spun by the wheel of fortune. High-stakes
gambling is the magnet attracting gaunt young novice
Jean (Mann) and voluble divorcee Jackie (Moreau),
who's well-accustomed to hustling the tables. For both,
gambling is an aphrodisiac and poison. Told with a brisk
step and a keen eye for detail, amid the Monte Carlo
and Nice locations, Demy's film is brilliantly lensed in
black and white by Jean Rabier, who captures the
seductive sparkle of casino life. Michel Legrand's esca-
lating, intoxicating score conveys the heady atmosphere
of a big casino win. Sporting a peroxide blonde rinse
and clad in figure-hugging Pierre Cardin outfits,
Moreau makes one of Demy's most memorable hero-
ines. *The Verdict:* 4/5 *Availability:* Region 1 DVD
(Wellspring) with clip from a Demy documentary,
trailer, filmographies and weblinks.

Baisers Volés (1968)

Alternative Title: *Stolen Kisses*

Directed by François Truffaut. Starring Jean–Pierre Léaud, Delphine Seyrig, Claude Jade. 91 mins.

The third film but second full-length feature in Truffaut's quasi-autobiographical saga about Antoine Doinel. Resembling Truffaut more and more as he grows older, Léaud resumes the main role as Antoine is discharged from the army, starts a brief career as a private investigator in Paris and falls in love with the wrong woman. Léaud is in fine form and Truffaut extracts plum performances from his supporting cast while directing with a simple, unadorned approach. There's also a refreshing sense of play throughout the picture. The result is a surprising snapshot of Parisian life in 1968, for there's no mention of the riots that rocked the city. The director dedicated the film to the head of the Cinémathèque, Henri Langlois. *The Verdict:* 3/5 *Availability:* VHS (Artificial Eye), deleted. All-regions DVD (Fox Lorber). Also part of Criterion's *The Adventures of Antoine Doinel Boxset* (Region 1 DVD).

La Belle Noiseuse (1991)

Alternative Title: *The Beautiful Troublemaker*

Directed by Jacques Rivette. Starring Michel Piccoli, Jane Birkin, Emmanuelle Béart. 229 mins.

A film about truth, beauty and magic. Rivette's spell-binding study of artistry follows a young woman (Béart) and her artist boyfriend (David Burszstein) as they visit a retired, reclusive painter (Piccoli) and his wife (Birkin) at their provincial abode. Béart sits for Piccoli and, as he paints her nude portrait, he becomes infatuated with her. Rivette doesn't rush himself and his film unfurls slowly and surely, before burning with an increasing intensity as the painter tries to bring the "invisible" out of his sitter. Taking its cue from a Balzac story, *La Belle Noiseuse* blooms with fine performances from Béart and veterans Birkin and Piccoli, who inhabits his role with customary ease. Rivette claimed Piccoli was the only actor in France who could play the part. It's tempting to say he's the only director who could fill a canvas of this size with such wondrous results. Limpid camerawork and lucid photography too, from William Lubtchansky. *The Verdict:* 4/5 *Availability:* Two-tape VHS (Artificial Eye) and two-disc DVD (Artificial Eye) including interviews with Rivette and the screenwriters.

Les Biches (1967)

Alternative Titles: *The Does, Bad Girls, Girlfriends*

Directed by Claude Chabrol. Starring Stéphane Audran, Jacqueline Sassard, Jean-Louis Trintignant. 99 mins.

Probably a popular rental for male cinéphiles in dirty macs, this lesbian thriller opens with a young street artist (Jacqueline Sassard) being picked up by an older woman named Frédérique (Stéphane Audran). The two soon become inseparable, as the artist is introduced to Frédérique's decadent life of leisure in St Tropez. Before long, however, their relationship is threatened by Paul (Trintignant, Audran's former husband) and the plot begins to twist and turn. There is little room for titillation in Chabrol's picture, which was co-written with the director's long-term collaborator Paul Gégauff. Pierre Jansen once again provides the sparse musical accompaniment and, in the lead roles, both Audran and Sassard show fine femme fatale form. *The Verdict:* 4/5 *Availability:* Region 0 DVD (Arrow) and VHS (Arrow).

Bob le Flambeur (1955)

Alternative Titles: *Bob the Gambler, Fever Heat*

Directed by Jean-Pierre Melville. Starring Roger Duchesne, Isabelle Corney, Daniel Cauchy. 100 mins.

Melville's crime movies typically came with a tip of the fedora to earlier American films. This caper about a retired bank robber who can't resist one more job is more than just a landmark film for the French New Wave – it's a classic contribution to the film noir genre. Shot by Claude Chabrol's regular cinematographer Henri Decaë, *Bob le Flambeur* is a supremely moody affair. Played to perfection by Roger Duchesne, the craggy Bob is an infamous, white-haired gangster who seems past his prime (yet commands respect throughout Montmartre) and tries to do his best by Paulo, his impressionable young pupil. A class act through and through, from Melville's own voice-over narration during the opening to the preparations for the Deauville casino heist and the stylised shoot-out sequence at the end – a palpable influence on *Bande à Part*. The screenplay, co-written by Melville and Auguste Le Breton (who also wrote Jules Dassin's heist classic *Rififi*), is solid gold. Witness Melville's use of the jump-cut several years before *A Bout de Souffle*. *The Verdict:* 5/5 *Availability:* Region 2 DVD (Warner), VHS (Warner) deleted.

Le Boucher (1970)

Alternative Title: *The Butcher*

Directed by Claude Chabrol. Starring Stéphane Audran, Jean Yanne, Antonio Passalia. 94 mins.

Chabrol was a master of the countryside crime film and *Le Boucher* is a village thriller *par excellence*. Popular school marm Hélène (an ice-blonde Audran) befriends butcher and war veteran Popaul (Jean Yanne) at a wedding but when a serial killer begins to pick off her female neighbours Hélène has doubts. Does this butcher have blood on his hands from the day job or from more sinister practices? Chabrol shot this engrossing film in Tremolet en Perigord and he shows a fine eye for locations, such as the woods where the first corpse is discovered and the eerie caves first glimpsed in the harrowing title sequence. He also keenly records the village's ceremonies, from the festivities of the opening wedding to a funeral in the rain. Pierre Jansen's discordant score tweaks the nerves and Yanne's performance – like Peter Lorre's in *M* – manages to tug at the heartstrings. Part of Chabrol's genius is that, in a film revolving around murder, the most powerful moment is a kiss. *The Verdict:* 4/5 *Availability:* Region 0 DVD (Arrow), VHS (Arrow).

La Boulangère de Monceau (1962)

Alternative Titles: *The Girl at the Monceau Bakery, The Baker of Monceau, The Baker's Girl of Monceau*

Directed by Eric Rohmer. Starring Barbet Schroeder, Fred Junk, Michèle Girardon. 26 mins.

The first of Rohmer's six moral tales, this 16mm short was the first film to be produced by his production company, Les Films du Losange. It introduces the theme of the series: the protagonist is enamoured with one woman, becomes sidetracked with another and then ends up with his original interest. The film's narrator remembers his youthful infatuation with a woman and his frequent trips to a local bakery. Shot on the streets of Paris, this is an atmospheric and often humorous tale and makes an interesting companion piece to Godard's early short, *Charlotte et Véronique, ou Tous les Garçons S'Apellent Patrick.* The main role is taken by producer Barbet Schroeder, but the narrator is actually film critic Bertrand Tavernier, shortly to make his own directorial debut. *The Verdict: 3/5 Availability:* All-regions DVD (Fox Lorber) including Rohmer's second moral tale, *La Carrière de Suzanne.* The two films are also on a VHS tape (Hendrig), deleted.

Les Carabiniers (1963)

Alternative Titles: *The Riflemen, The Soldiers*

Directed by Jean-Luc Godard. Starring Albert Juross, Marino Mase, Catherine Ribeiro. 80 mins.

The ultimate anti-war movie: a work that's both anti-war and anti-war movies in the conventional sense. Based on a play by Benjamino Joppolo, Godard's bold, bitter picture is shot through with a sardonic streak of humour. The film opens with riflemen recruiting two poor brothers, Michelangelo and Ulysses, into the king's army with promises of unlimited riches. "In war," the brothers are told, "anything goes." Excited by the prospect of a carte blanche to kill and steal at will, they pick up arms. Inspired by Eisenstein's montages, the film inter-cuts the rampages of these Keystone Soldiers with archive war footage and postcards from the front line ("bodies, decay, rot, death, etc" reads one). Marino Mase plays Ulysses with the stubble-and-cigar pose of a gung-ho action hero, while Albert Juross makes Michelangelo a goofy, sweaty schoolboy with a comic book in one hand and a rifle in the other. The film has the same grainy look as Roberto Rossellini's neorealist feature *Rome, Open City*; Rossellini himself was one of the co-writers. The film's condemnation of the military's abuse of power remains as relevant as ever. *The Verdict:* 4/5 *Availability:* Region 1 DVD (Fox Lorber) with an abridged audio commentary from David Sterritt.

Le Cercle Rouge (1970)

Alternative Title: *The Red Circle*

Directed by Jean-Pierre Melville. Starring Alain Delon, Gian Maria Volonté, Yves Montand. 136 mins.

Another stylish heist thriller from Melville, this has

been championed by countless directors, from Quentin Tarantino to Pedro Almodóvar. The film follows three crooks hitting a jewellers. The operation is led by *Le Samouraï* himself, Alain Delon, wrapped in a trench coat and sporting a bushy 'tache. Then there's Yves Montand (soon to appear in Godard's *Tout Va Bien*) and Gian Maria Volonté (who played redoubtable, scowling rogues in Sergio Leone's first two 'Dollars' films). The film's opening memorably crosscuts between Delon's release from prison and Volonté's escape from a speeding train, as he gives police inspector André Bourvil the slip. Melville has you eating out of his hand from here on in. The film features some excellent locations, and the director shows himself to be equally at home with the woodland terrain, where the film opens and ends, and the city's mean streets. Actions often speak louder than words in Melville's films and *Rififi* fans will savour the silent heist sequence. A cold, direct and devilishly clever work. *The Verdict:* 5/5 *Availability:* Region 2 DVD (BFI) with commentary and an insightful introduction from Ginette Vincendeau. The BFI has also released Melville's *Le Doulos, Les Enfants Terribles* and *Léon Morin, Prêtre*.

Cléo de 5 à 7 (1962)

Alternative Title: *Cleo from 5 to 7*

Directed by Agnès Varda. Starring Corinne Marchand, Antoine Bourseiller, Dorothée Blank. 90 mins.

A former shutterbug for the Théâtre National Populaire (TNP), Agnès Varda is the only female director commonly associated with the New Wave. Many credit her 1955 short *La Pointe Courte*, made when she was 26, as a forerunner to the movement. Presented in 'real time', her pleasing feature *Cléo de 5 à 7* follows a singer who is waiting for the result of some medical tests, over a two-hour period of her life. The film is considerably influenced by *Lola* (Varda was married to Jacques Demy) and features cameos from newly-weds Anna Karina and Jean-Luc Godard, the ubiquitous Jean-Claude Brialy, Sami Frey and Eddie Constantine, soon to appear in *Alphaville*. *The Verdict:* 4/5 *Availability:* VHS (Momentum) and Region 1 DVD (Criterion).

Conte de Printemps (1989)

Alternative Title: *A Tale of Springtime*

Directed by Eric Rohmer. Starring Anne Teyssèdre, Hugues Quester, Florence Darel. 103 mins.

After his moral tales and comedies and proverbs, Rohmer began a new film cycle in the late 1980s, this time based around the four seasons. The first feature, *Conte de Printemps*, is an entertaining affair revolving around a teacher, Jeanne, who befriends a precocious student, Natasha, at a party. The pair become unlikely flatmates for a period as Natasha attempts to set up her new friend with her father. Told with Rohmer's usual languid pace and observant style, the film offers a virtual inventory of the director's tropes: chance meetings and fledgling friendships, the contrast between the sexes and between different generations, wide-ranging artistic debate and scenes set around domestic gatherings. Natasha is a quintessential Rohmer heroine. She speaks for many of his characters when she says, "Even if I'm idle, thinking keeps me busy." *The Verdict:* 4/5 *Availability:* VHS (Artificial Eye), Region 1 DVD (MGM/UA).

Les Demoiselles de Rochefort (1967)

Alternative Title: *The Young Girls of Rochefort*

Directed by Jacques Demy. Starring Catherine Deneuve, Françoise Dorléac, Gene Kelly. 125 mins.

Another bright and breezy spin through Demy-ville with dancing sailors, fairground fun, candyfloss colours and bittersweet songs. Plus, there's Deneuve and Dorléac playing twins and the casting coup of Gene Kelly. The Garnier sisters have aspirations beyond their environs and are destined for Paris; when the fair comes to Rochefort it brings George Chakiris and Grover Dale, who want the girls for their act but Deneuve has her eyes on Jacques Perrin and Dorléac falls for music maestro Kelly. This is characteristically rapturous stuff from Demy who considered the film a homage to life. He draws likeable turns from his stars and deftly juggles the love stories with eye-catching results. It's worth watching if only for the sisters' foot-tapping signature song. See if you can spot Agnès Varda in her cameo role as a nun. *The Verdict:* 3/5 *Availability:* VHS (Momentum) and Region 1 DVD (Miramax).

Le Dernier Métro (1980)

Alternative Title: *The Last Metro*

Directed by François Truffaut. Starring Catherine Deneuve, Gérard Depardieu, Jean Poiret. 126 mins.

It could be said that Truffaut's *Le Dernier Métro* does for the theatre what his *La Nuit Américaine* did for the cinema. A backstage costume drama often reminiscent of Ernst Lubitsch's *To Be or Not to Be*, the film is surprisingly close to the 'cinéma de papa' that Truffaut derided in his youth. Deneuve and Depardieu excel in the lead roles. In a part written specifically for her, Deneuve plays the wife of Lucas Steiner, a successful Jewish theatre director who is forced to go into hiding during the Nazis' Occupation of France in 1942. Depardieu is the promising young actor who arrives from the Grand Guignol to star in Steiner's new production, put on in the director's apparent absence. Truffaut's film cleaned up at the Césars in 1981. *The Verdict:* 4/5 *Availability:* VHS (Tartan) and Region 2 DVD (Tartan) with Truffaut interview, commentary from historian Jean-Pierre Azema and other extras.

Détective (1985)

Directed by Jean-Luc Godard. Starring Nathalie Baye, Claude Brasseur, Johnny Hallyday. 95 mins.

Who else but Godard could cast Johnny Hallyday in a metaphysical thriller dedicated to Clint Eastwood and John Cassavetes, with music by Liszt, Chopin and Wagner and references that run from Shakespeare to

Poverty Row B-movies? With an opening nod to his own *Sauve Qui Peut (La Vie)* – a woman's movements reduced to slow motion on a surveillance tape – Godard constructs the scaffolding for a whodunit revolving around a murder in a Parisian hotel. The guests include a boxer preparing for a prize fight, complete with unconventional entourage, and a pilot whose marriage is taking a nosedive. Brasseur and Baye are in fine form; Jeanne-Pierre Léaud and a young Julie Delpy co-star. *The Verdict: 3/5 Availability:* Region 2 DVD (Optimum) with filmed introduction by Colin MacCabe.

Domicile Conjugal (1970)

Alternative Title: *Bed and Board*

Directed by François Truffaut. Starring Jean-Pierre Léaud, Claude Jade, Hiroko Berghauer. 95 mins.

Truffaut's fourth Antoine Doinel film is possibly the weakest of the series. Antoine as adult, with wife and child, embroiled in an extramarital affair and suffering from a mid-life crisis simply isn't as engrossing as Antoine the adolescent. The director intended the film to be in the style of the great American comedies by the likes of Lubitsch, but the result is a rather lacklustre affair. *The Verdict: 2/5 Availability:* Part of Criterion's *The Adventures of Antoine Doinel* boxset (Region 1 DVD) and also on a Region 1 DVD from Fox Lorber. VHS (Artificial Eye), deleted.

La Femme de L'Aviateur (1980)

Alternative Title: *The Aviator's Wife*

Directed by Eric Rohmer. Starring Philippe Marlaud, Marie Rivière, Anne-Laure Meury. 106 mins.

Although less radical and polemical than Jean-Luc Godard or Jacques Rivette, Eric Rohmer also has a tendency to divide audiences. Viewers either embrace his unhurried, thoughtful films or grow frustrated waiting for something to happen. The first of his series of comedies and proverbs, this is a typically light-hearted and ultimately elusive feature from Rohmer. Postal worker François becomes intrigued by his girl-friend's former lover and begins to play detective, following him around town. During his impromptu investigations he meets a woman who is bemused by his behaviour. Later comedies and proverbs include *Le Beau Mariage*, *Le Rayon Vert* and *L'Ami de Mon Amie*. *The Verdict: 3/5 Availability:* VHS (Arrow) and Region 0 DVD (Arrow) with trailer and Rohmer's thoughts on the film.

La Femme Infidèle (1968)

Alternative Title: *The Unfaithful Wife*

Directed by Claude Chabrol. Starring Stéphane Audran, Michel Bouquet, Maurice Ronet. 98 mins.

The first of a number of stylish psychological thrillers, often referred to as the Hélène cycle, this sees the unhappily married Audran embark on an affair with Ronet, leading hubby Bouquet to wreak revenge. The scene in which he visits his wife's lover is breath-taking; Ronet shares a whiskey with Bouquet and shows him around his apartment, even leading him to the bedroom where he's been cuckolded. Bouquet plays the observer brilliantly, his smallest expressions and gestures are perfect as his suspicions grow, before his contained frustration and fury finally explode. The film has some delicious Hitchcockian touches – witness the inopportune timing of Bouquet's traffic accident. As always with Chabrol, there are some entertaining minor characters, including Ronet's simpering short-skirted secretary and the private eye he hires to follow his wife. Audran excels in the lead role, and Diane Lane did a fine job in Adrian Lyne's 2002 re-imagining, *Unfaithful*. *The Verdict:* 5/5 *Availability:* VHS (Arrow) and Region 0 DVD (Arrow).

Les Glaneurs et la Glaneuse (2000)

Alternative Title: *The Gleaners and I*

Directed by Agnès Varda. Starring Agnès Varda, Edouard Loubet, Louis Pons. 82 mins.

This well-received DV documentary is everything we've come to expect from Agnès Varda: warm, witty, irreverent and extremely personal. "To glean," we're told at the start of her film, "is to gather after the harvest." However, the efficiency of modern machinery has rendered this traditional farming practice largely redundant. Varda makes a genial host as she sets out cross-country to explore the modern face of gleaning.

On the road she meets those who glean as a business practice (chef Edouard Loubet), for artistic purposes (painter Louis Pons) or simply as a means of survival (the unnamed figures scavenging the streets like magpies for items to salvage). Each gleaner has his or her own reasons and Varda draws frank, intimate revelations from her subjects. The booty is varied: berries plucked from forgotten vineyards, fridges rescued from the roadside and all manner of ingredients from the rubbish bin. The ingenuity on display matches that of a contemporary American documentary, Marc Singer's *Dark Days*. *The Verdict:* 5/5 *Availability:* Region 1 DVD (Zeitgeist) with production notes and Varda's 60-minute sequel, *The Gleaners and I: Two Years Later*.

Jacquot de Nantes (1991)

Alternative Title: *Jacquot*

Directed by Agnès Varda. Starring Philippe Maron, Edouard Joubeaud, Jacques Demy. 118 mins.

Varda's affectionate and undeniably moving tribute to her husband Jacques Demy is a scrapbook of songs, movies and memories. It is predominantly a dramatisation of the early life of the film-maker, portrayed at varying ages by three different actors. This narrative is intercut both with clips from Demy's own films and home footage of the director before his death. Demy remembers his childhood in France during the Occupation and we observe his love of puppetry and first experiences with the cinema, in the shape of Disney animations and the collaborative works of

Prévert and Carné. *The Verdict:* 4/5 *Availability:* VHS (Tartan) and NTSC (Columbia Tristar).

La Jetée (1962)

Alternative Title: *The Pier*

Directed by Chris Marker. Starring Jean Négroni, Hélène Chatelain, Davos Hanich. 28 mins.

Made in 1962, but not released until 1964, *La Jetée* is writer and documentary-maker Marker's only fictional film. Winner of the prestigious Prix Jean Vigo, this story of a time traveller is written, directed and photographed by Marker and composed almost completely of still photographs. It is famous for influencing Terry Gilliam's *Twelve Monkeys* and can be seen as an especially interesting companion piece to the work of Alain Resnais. *The Verdict:* 4/5 *Availability:* VHS (Nouveau Pictures) and available on a Region 2 DVD double feature with *Sans Soleil* (Nouveau Pictures), including short Marker documentary, *Chris on Chris*.

Made in USA (1966)

Directed by Jean-Luc Godard. Starring Anna Karina, Jean-Pierre Léaud, Laszlo Szabo. 85 mins.

Godard dedicated this colourful concoction, which was filmed concurrently with the sociological essay *Deux ou Trois Choses Que Je Sais D'Elle*, to Samuel Fuller and Nicholas Ray. Those nods, combined with the fact that there are characters named Richard Widmark and David Goodis, might lead you to expect a certain shade of noir. The film recalls the old maxim, that all you need to make a movie is a girl and a gun, but ultimately Godard is more interested in ideas than action. In the opening scene, Karina's heroine strikes an old man dead with her shoe and likens her story to "a Walt Disney film starring Humphrey Bogart." Karina takes the Bogey role – or the Constantine role – as the movie revolves around the mystery of her former lover's death. Whisking together wordplay, physical comedy and political debate, *Made in USA* is sparky stuff with a typically Godardian sense of humour. All this plus Marianne Faithfull singing 'As Tears Go By'. *The Verdict:* 3/5 *Availability:* Part of Warner's Jean-Luc Godard DVD Collection: Volume 2 (Region 2), which also includes *Prénom Carmen* and *Pierrot le Fou*.

Ma Nuit Chez Maud (1969)

Alternative Title: *My Night at Maud's*

Directed by Eric Rohmer. Starring Jean-Louis Trintignant, Françoise Fabian, Marie-Christine Barrault. 113 mins.

The third of Rohmer's six moral tales, *Ma Nuit Chez Maud* was nominated for Academy Awards® for Best Foreign Film and Best Screenplay. Memorably shot by Cuban cinematographer Nestor Almendros, the film is slow paced to say the least. Jean-Louis Trintignant is the detached provincial engineer who, through a mutual friend, meets the intoxicating and beautiful recluse Maud (Françoise Fabian) on a winter night. The couple discuss love (she is divorced, he has never married) and

Catholicism (he is religious, she isn't) at great length in Maud's apartment and then fall asleep in the same bed. By morning, the engineer's life has changed. *The Verdict:* 4/5 *Availability:* VHS (Connoisseur), deleted. Region 1 DVD (Fox Lorber).

Masculin Féminin (1966)

Alternative Title: *Masculine-Feminine*

Directed by Jean-Luc Godard. Starring Jean-Pierre Léaud, Chantal Goya, Catherine-Isabelle Duport. 110 mins.

Godard's radical study-in-sketches of the "children of Marx and Coca-Cola" follows young lovers Paul, who has just completed his military service, and Madeleine, an aspiring pop star. The film reveals the director's developing interest in sound, slogans and social issues, all of which would come to the fore in his second outing with actor Léaud, *La Chinoise*. Both features are concerned with Vietnam and both examine the impact of the interview technique. *Masculin Féminin* is a slightly more uneven affair than its follow-up, yet has a refreshingly mischievous sense of humour throughout. Brigitte Bardot makes a brief cameo appearance. *The Verdict:* 3/5 *Availability:* VHS (Nouveau Pictures) and Region 2 DVD (Nouveau Pictures) with booklet and gallery.

Merci Pour le Chocolat (2000)

Alternative Title: *Nightcap*

Directed by Claude Chabrol. Starring Isabelle Huppert, Jacques Dutronc, Anna Mouglalis. 97 mins.

To borrow from the title of one of Chabrol's later films, Huppert plays a 'flower of evil' in this deliberately ambiguous, slow-burning thriller. She's Mika, the step-mother who may or may not have bumped off her best friend in order to steal back her husband and who might just be poisoning her stepson with her famous homemade drinking chocolate. Anna Mouglalis plays the amateur sleuth investigating these proceedings, drawn into the affair through a tenuous connection to Mika's husband. Chabrol deftly folds together an array of parent-child relationships (surrogate or absent parents, substituted or neglected children) and cranks up the tension towards an edge-of-seat climax. Reuniting with her *Slow Motion* co-star Jacques Dutronc and appearing in her sixth film for Chabrol, Huppert is perfectly cast as Mika, shielding sadism beneath her smile. Shot in Lausanne, Switzerland. *The Verdict:* 4/5 *Availability:* Region 2 DVD (Artificial Eye) with behind-the-scenes documentary, Huppert inter-view, Mouglalis screen test and other appetizing extras.

More (1969)

Directed by Barbet Schroeder. Starring Mimsy Farmer, Klaus Grünberg, Heinz Engelmann. 111 mins.

Former *Cahiers* critic Barbet Schroeder played an

integral role in the New Wave, producing Rohmer's fledgling works among others. He made his own assured directorial debut at the fag end of the 1960s with this extraordinary experimental film, co-written with Chabrol's regular scribe Paul Gégauff. Klaus Grünberg plays the German Stefan, who cuts loose after finishing his studies and hitches a ride to Paris, where he becomes besotted with an American hippy, Estelle, who he meets in the city's druggy subculture. Stefan gets his first high with Estelle but, as the action shifts to Ibiza, their romance turns sour and he turns to harder drugs. Schroeder's film is one bad trip. It's as much a touchstone and a time capsule of the era as the same year's *Easy Rider* and *Midnight Cowboy* and prefigures the director's later *Barfly* in its depiction of doomed, destructive relationships. Pink Floyd provide the soundtrack. *The Verdict:* 3/5 *Availability:* Region 2 DVD (BFI) includes an interview with the director. The BFI has also released Schroeder's *Maîtresse* (1976) on DVD.

La Nuit Américaine (1973)

Alternative Title: *Day for Night*

Directed by François Truffaut. Starring Jacqueline Bisset, Valentina Cortese, Jean-Pierre Léaud. 116 mins.

Dedicated to silent screen sisters Lilian and Dorothy Gish, Truffaut's highly autobiographical study of film-making is a delight from start to finish. He himself stars as the director of a tawdry romantic drama called *Je Vous Présente Pamela*, which is dogged by the usual behind-the-scenes shenanigans. Bisset is the fragile beauty with emotional problems, Léaud the immature actor she becomes involved with and Cortese the prima donna beyond her prime. Fine ensemble acting, stylish direction, humorous and telling insights into Truffaut's work and another fine score from Georges Delerue make it well worth a repeat viewing. *The Verdict:* 5/5 *Availability:* VHS (Warner), deleted. Region 1 DVD (Warner) with documentaries and Truffaut interviews.

Paris vu Par... (1964)

Alternative Title: *Six in Paris*

Collection of six short films, directed by Jean-Daniel Pollet, Jean Rouch, Jean Douchet, Eric Rohmer, Jean-Luc Godard, Claude Chabrol. 95 mins.

One of a number of compilations of shorts (called *films à sketch* by the French) that proved popular in the 1960s, this collaborative New Wave film actually succeeds in telling us surprisingly little about Paris. *Paris vu Par...* is notable, in particular, for Rouch's domestic drama *Gare du Nord*, which was shot in two takes, and Pollet's humorous *Rue Saint Denis*. In his contribution, *Montparnasse-Levallois*, Godard tells a story previously recounted by Belmondo's character in *Une Femme est Une Femme*. *The Verdict:* 2/5 *Availability:* VHS (Connoisseur), deleted.

Le Petit Soldat (1960)

Alternative Title: *The Little Soldier*

Directed by Jean-Luc Godard. Starring Michel Subor, Anna Karina, Henri-Jacques Huet. 88 mins.

Michel Subor plays secret agent Bruno, who hides out in Geneva at the time of the conflict in Algiers. He deliberates over a deadly assignment and turns his attention to Anna Karina's model Véronica. *Le Petit Soldat* was filmed in 1960 but wasn't screened until 1963 (and even then in an edited state) due to its contentious treatment of Algiers. The film is known for its infamous torture sequences but there are lighter shades here too. The scene in which Bruno and Véronica shuffle around an apartment playing games and discussing the arts, as he tries to woo her into bed, directly flashes back to *A Bout de Souffle*. In their first film together, one can already get a sense of how Godard will create an icon out of his leading lady, as Karina poses and dances in these sequences. Incidentally, it's in this film that Subor voices the oft-quoted maxim that "cinema is truth 24 times a second." *The Verdict:* 3/5 *Availability:* Part of Warner's Jean-Luc Godard DVD Collection (Region 2) which also includes *Une Femme est Une Femme* and *Alphaville*.

CHRIS WIEGAND

Que la Bête Meure (1969)

Alternative Titles: *The Beast Must Die, This Man Must Die, Killer!*

Directed by Claude Chabrol. Starring Michel Duchaussoy, Caroline Cellier, Jean Yanne. 110 mins.

Quintessential Chabrol: a chilling thriller that's as crisp as its wintry Brittany setting. When a young child is killed in a hit-and-run incident, his distraught father (Duchaussoy) sets out to seek revenge on the motorist responsible, eventually infiltrating his family. Like the cuckolded husband in Chabrol's *La Femme Infidèle*, the father's obsessive quest steadily and completely consumes him, his descent to hell recorded in detail in a vivid diary of hate. From the stunning opening sequence onwards, this makes riveting viewing and reveals a director who is in complete control of his material. Chabrol just doesn't miss a beat. *The Verdict:* 4/5 *Availability:* VHS (Arrow) and Region 1 DVD (Pathfinder).

RoGoPaG (1962)

Alternative Title: *Let's Have a Brainwash*

Collection of four short films directed by Roberto Rossellini, Ugo Gregoretti, Pier Paolo Pasolini, Jean-Luc Godard. 122 mins.

An ensemble of short films from ROssellini, GOdard, PAsolini and Gregoretti, *RoGoPaG* announces its collective theme as "the jolly onset of the world's end." Rossellini's *Illibatezza* (*Chastity*) is a light-hearted study of sex and celluloid, concerning an Italian air stewardess who is pursued by an overeager American admirer. Pasolini's *La Ricotta* (*Curd Cheese*) stars a low-key Orson Welles as a movie director making a picture about the Crucifixion. Of the four films, Godard's contribution – the eerie *Il Nuovo Mondo* (*The New World*) – fits the bill best. It tells of a man whose relationship with his lover suffers from an atomic explosion above Paris. The most intriguing short, however, is from Gregoretti, whose satirical and irreverent *Il Pollo Ruspante* (*The Free-Range Chicken*) intercuts the study of a family consumed by consumerism, with a lecture delivered via voice-box from a noted professor. *The Verdict:* 3/5 *Availability:* VHS (Tartan).

Le Samouraï (1967)

Alternative Title: *The Godson*

Directed by Jean-Pierre Melville. Starring Alain Delon, François Perier, Nathalie Delon. 105 mins.

Melville's much-praised 1960s noir is a minimalist masterpiece. Alain Delon plays Jef Costello, a laconic hit man and lone wolf who is hunted down by the police after a nightclub murder. Benefiting from a sinister score and a great script, *Le Samouraï* is about as stylised as they come. This is a slow-paced, stark and under-stated meditation on solitude and honour that also frequently reveals itself to be the prototype of many modern American thrillers. Costello casts a sorrowful and sympathetic shadow over the hit man's usual milieu, from the faceless hotel rooms to underground gambling dens and smoky jazz clubs, all of which are memorably shot in a steely tone that matches the killer's eyes. *The Verdict:* 5/5 *Availability:* VHS (Artificial Eye), deleted.

Sauve Qui Peut (La Vie) (1980)

Alternative Title: *Slow Motion*

Directed by Jean-Luc Godard. Starring Isabelle Huppert, Jacques Dutronc, Nathalie Baye. 84 mins.

Shot in Switzerland, this beguiling, often absurd drama was heralded as Godard's return to mainstream film-making. Sporting specs and floppy fringe, Jacques Dutronc stars as a TV director named Paul Godard whose life is in tatters. Estranged from his wife and daughter – and recently separated from his girlfriend (a César-winning Baye) – Paul spends the night with a prostitute (Huppert) who's in trouble with her pimp. In marked contrast to the hop, skip and jumpcut style of his first film, Jean-Luc Godard here uses stop motion to lend poetic weight to selected episodes, whether inconsequential or dramatically pivotal. Twinned with Gabriel Yared's haunting score, sequences such as Baye cycling through the countryside are a wonder to behold. If the film seems fragmented or disjointed at first, it ultimately rewards the viewer with a rich, endlessly fascinating experience. The title sequence announces "un film composé par Jean-Luc Godard", hinting at the aural experiments at work. Lots to enjoy and unravel here. *The Verdict:* 3/5 *Availability:* VHS (Artificial Eye).

Triple Agent (2003)

Directed by Eric Rohmer. Starring Serge Renko, Katerina Didaskalou, Cyrielle Clair. 115 mins.

Since finishing his seasonal tales with 1998's *Conte D'Automne*, Rohmer has helmed two handsome period pieces. He trained his expert eye on the French Revolution with *L'Anglaise et le Duc* and then turned in this slow-burning espionage drama set in Paris, in the run-up to the Second World War. Both films reveal consummate recreation of the era, through sets and costumes (and in the case of the former, lyrical digital trickery) but are just as effective in capturing the turbulent mood of the time. Above all else, *Triple Agent* is a film about loyalty. The film announces itself as a fiction spun from a real-life, unresolved mystery. Katerina Didaskalou is superb as a Greek artist who begins to question the political beliefs of her husband of 12 years, Fyodor (Serge Renko). Punctuating the tale with archival newsreel material, Rohmer wraps his characteristic incidental delights and customary debate inside a thriller plot with impressive results. *The Verdict:* 3/5 *Availability:* Region 2 DVD (Artificial Eye) with historical featurette and trailer.

Viva Maria (1965)

Alternative Title: *Viva Maria!*

Directed by Louis Malle. Starring Jeanne Moreau, Brigitte Bardot, George Hamilton. 120 mins.

This frothy comedy-cum-adventure movie had the

mouth-watering partnership of Bardot and Moreau as fun-loving strippers both named Maria. Moreau recruits Bardot for her music-hall troupe and the pair spark some revolutionary mischief on the road in Central America. It's over-long and half-baked but if the results are uneven, the stars are unquestionably sexy. The contrast between the leading ladies is fascinating and there are some standout scenes. In their first routine together, Bardot bursts out of her costume and Moreau, not to be outdone, starts to shed her own clothes – cue a stripping contest which leaves the conductor gobsmacked and the orchestra ground to a halt. When the film was released, after a string of largely unfounded rumours about on-set bitching between the two stars, it proved a huge success in Europe. Moreau won a BAFTA award for her performance. *The Verdict:* 2/5 *Availability:* Currently unavailable on DVD or VHS.

Week-End (1967)

Alternative Titles: *Weekend, Le Week-End*

Directed by Jean-Luc Godard. Starring Mireille Darc, Jean Yanne, Jean-Pierre Kalfon. 103 mins.

An apocalyptic satire on consumerism and the bour-geoisie that signals "the end of cinema" and the start of Godard's political film-making phase, *Week-End* was famously filmed in a series of extremely long takes and is notable for the extraordinary opening traffic jam sequence. Truffaut regular Jean-Pierre Léaud and Godard's second wife Anne Wiazemsky co-star, alongside Chabrol's regular scriptwriting collaborator Paul Gégauff. Experimental, cerebral, provocative stuff. *The Verdict:* 3/5 *Availability:* Region 2 DVD (Artificial Eye) includes interview with Coutard and Mike Figgis' comments on the film. VHS (Connoisseur), deleted.

Les Yeux Sans Visage (1959)

Alternative Title: *Eyes Without a Face*

Directed by Georges Franju. Starring Pierre Brasseur, Alida Valli, Edith Scob. 90 mins.

Co-founder of the Cinémathèque Française, Georges Franju was greatly influenced by the German expressionist directors of the 1930s and their mark is more than apparent in this surreal, freaky feature. A cult favourite, it tells the highly unpleasant story of a girl whose visage is mutilated in a car crash and whose father sets about getting his hands on a replacement face for her. Not for the squeamish. *The Verdict:* 3/5 *Availability:* VHS (Connoisseur), Region 1 DVD (Criterion).

Reference Material

French New Wave by Jean Douchet. Distribute Art Publishers, 1999. The daddy of all New Wave resources, this is a comprehensive, stylish and lavishly illustrated coffee table book written by one of the lesser-known figures of the movement. Douchet wrote for *Cahiers* and directed one of the best short films in the collaborative New Wave project *Paris vu Par...* He intelligently divides his book into a series of chapters that examine topics such as 'the studio,' 'the street' and 'the body,' as well as offering in-depth technical information and historical analysis.

The French New Wave: An Artistic School by Michel Marie. Blackwell Publishing, 2003. You can't fault Michel Marie's account of the movement's origins, intentions and impact, all of which are clearly laid out in a step-by-step fashion. Marie quickly sets the scene of French society in the 1950s, charts the media's role in heralding the New Wave and vividly contrasts the New Wave style with the 'tradition de qualité'. He then follows the movement through to 1963, with a glance forward to those later film-makers inspired by the movement. The author has dug deep into box-office records, production costs and pivotal news articles, resulting in a thorough, rigorous study furnished with useful lists and timelines.

A History of the French New Wave Cinema by Richard Neupert. The University of Wisconsin Press, 2002. Chabrol, Truffaut and Godard share the main focus of this highly readable guide but Neupert also gives sensitive and passionate assessments of the lesser-known work of Alexandre Astruc, Agnès Varda, Jacques Doniol-Valcroze and Pierre Kast. This history is particularly strong on the world of ciné-clubs and film journals from which the main directors sprung. Neupert delivers fascinating details from the films' production histories and gives a nuanced analysis of the pictures themselves. Thoroughly recommended.

French Cinema Since 1950 by Emma Wilson. Rowman & Littlefield Publishers, 1999. An engrossing and wide-ranging study of French film in the second half of the 20th century, Wilson's book is a 'history of cinema as love story.' It features commentaries on several New Wave films, including *A Bout de Souffle*, *Hiroshima Mon Amour* and *Les Quatre Cents Coups* and also discusses later films such as Jean-Jacques Beineix's *Betty Blue*, Luc Besson's *Nikita* and Claude Berri's *Jean de Florette* and *Manon des Sources*.

Contemporary French Cinema by Guy Austin. Manchester University Press, 1996. Focusing more on the New New Wave than the New Wave, this contemporary study features some enlightening analyses of films by Resnais, Rivette and Varda, as well as those of the 'cinéma du look' directors (Beineix, Carax and Besson). Other films profiled include *Delicatessen*, *Les Valseuses* and *Emmanuelle*.

French Cinema: A Student's Guide by Phil Powrie and Keith Reader. Hodder Arnold, 2002. An informative primer on French cinema in general, from Lumière and Méliès to Kassovitz and Jeunet, this guide features a perceptive appraisal of the directors and theorists of the New Wave. The book comes with a selection of essays on key French films, including an analysis of the famous opening sequence of Godard's *Week-End*. There's a useful list of César and Prix Louis Delluc award-winners and the authors point towards a wealth of other recommended French texts.

Godard: A Portrait of the Artist at 70 by Colin MacCabe. Bloomsbury, 2003. MacCabe's achievement, in distilling Godard's lengthy career and enormous oeuvre into an extremely readable 400-odd pages, must be applauded. MacCabe offers valuable background information on the director's childhood, captures the heady Cinémathèque days and assesses his pivotal collaborations with Anna Karina and Anne-Marie Miéville. The book bustles with the author's own personal recollections of both the work and the man himself. There are some wonderful illustrations too, from *Cahiers* covers to behind-the-scenes snaps.

Jean-Luc Godard: Interviews edited by David Sterritt. US: University Press of Mississippi, 1998. This collection of interviews with Godard spans the director's entire career. The earliest interview is from 1962 and is conducted by Tom Milne at the time of the release of *Vivre sa Vie*. The next, a lengthy interview with Gene Youngblood, is taken from the end of the 1960s. The final interview was held in 1996. While there may not be a wealth of material on the main films featured in this Pocket Essential, there is plenty of wide-ranging discussion on Godard's later work.

Godard on Godard translated and edited by Tom Milne. Da Capo Press, 1972. This volume of Godard's criticism offers some enlightening views, both on the young critic's cinematic heroes and on the young director's first movies. Much of the criticism is from the pages of *Cahiers*, and there is an in-depth interview with Godard from the December 1962 issue of the journal. Other highlights include a commentary on *Une Femme est Une Femme* (as well as the film's original scenario) and some illuminating material on *Pierrot le Fou*.

François Truffaut: Letters translated and edited by Gilbert Adair. Faber and Faber, 1989. A massive collection of Truffaut's correspondence from 1945 to 1984. The material ranges from childhood letters to his best friend Robert Lachenay, to personal accounts to Helen Scott, notes to collaborators such as Charles Aznavour and Marcel Moussy, and discussions of the film-making craft to the likes of Louis Malle and Alfred Hitchcock. This invaluable look into the personal and professional life of Truffaut has a foreword written by Godard and includes the evidence of the two film-makers' infamous falling out.

François Truffaut by Diana Holmes and Robert Ingram. Manchester University Press, 1998. This thoroughly researched academic study is part of a series of critiques on French film-makers, that includes commentaries on Luc Besson, Agnès Varda and Coline Serreau. Holmes and Ingram offer both biographical and thematic analyses of Truffaut's canon, looking at the representation of both mother and father figures and assessing the films in terms of genre.

François Truffaut by Annette Insdorf. Cambridge University Press, 1994. An extremely readable guide to the life and career of Truffaut. Insdorf examines the relation of his films to his main film-making influences, including Alfred Hitchcock and Jean Renoir. Her analysis of the Doinel films and the late 1960s thrillers is particularly astute.

Claude Chabrol by Guy Austin. Manchester University Press, 1999. Part of the same series on French film directors as Diana Holmes and Robert Ingram's study on François Truffaut. Described as 'the first book-length study of Chabrol to be published in English since 1970,' its detailed analysis of five decades of Chabrol's films brings home the director's prolific performance, from *Le Beau Serge* through to his numerous thrillers and literary adaptations. An intelligent, engaging guide to the director with useful observations on symbolism, genre and music in Chabrol's films. Definitely recommended.

Malle on Malle edited by Philip French. Faber and Faber, 1996. Described by French as a journey through the director's career, this invaluable addition to the successful Faber directors' series is made up of a series of illuminating conversations that took place, for the main part, between the editor and the film-maker in his house near Limogne-en-Quercy. A closing interview between Malle and the production assistant Oren Moverman on *Vanya on 42nd Street* brings the book right up to date, making this an essential guide to the director.

Chris Marker: Memories of the Future by Catherine Lupton. Reaktion Books, 2005. Lupton's book on Chris Marker is as intelligent and thought-provoking as the great director's films. Marker emerges as a master of many media here. The book combines a close analysis of Marker's works with plenty of anecdotal and biographical detail. Learn about Marker's early days as an essayist for *Esprit*, his collaborations with Alain Resnais in the 1950s, his involvement with the Group of Thirty (whose members included Agnès Varda) and the making of his famous films *Le Joli Mai* and *La Jetée* as well as lesser-known projects.

Bardot: An Intimate Portrait by Jeffrey Robinson. Penguin Books USA, 1996. An account of Bardot's life, from her strict upbringing, to her appearance on the front cover of *Elle* at the age of 14 and emergence as a barefooted screen siren, through to her retirement as an animal-loving recluse. Divided into two 'lives' and endorsed by BB herself, it features quotes from first-hand interviews with Bardot, Roger Vadim and Jeanne Moreau to name just a few.

The New Wave on the Web

http://www.bbc.co.uk/bbcfour

I have contributed several reviews of New Wave films to BBC Four's website as well as a profile of Jeanne Moreau and an interview with Philip French about Louis Malle.

http://www.bfi.org.uk/features/godard

The British Film Institute's mini-site for the 2001 Godard season includes biographical material, criticism, further links and a Q&A with Anna Karina from her onstage interview at the National Film Theatre.

http://www.cinemathequefrancaise.com
The online home for Langlois and Franju's Cinémathèque Française includes news, programme information and an essay on the role played by the cinema.

http://www.forevergodard.com
A stylish and fascinating site profiling the book *For Ever
Godard*, inspired by the Tate's 2001 event of the same
name. Contains a rich array of essays and images.

http://www.frenchculture.org
This site from New York's Cultural Services of the
French Embassy contains a wealth of up-to-date infor-
mation on French cinema past and present.

**http://www.guardian.co.uk/arts/story/0,,61161
6,00.html**
An entertaining and rather irreverent interview with
actor Jean-Claude Brialy, conducted in 2001.

**http://www.moviemaker.com/issues/47/french
new.html**
The American magazine *MovieMaker* offers a solid
tribute to the New Wave, with love letters from talents
including Mike Figgis, Tom Tykwer and Jean-Jacques
Annaud.

**http://www.thenation.com/doc.mhtml%3Fi=20
000131&s=bromley**
A lengthy account of the New Wave written by Carol
Bromley for New York's *The Nation*, sparked by the
release of Jean Douchet's book and a tome on Truffaut.

http://archive.salon.com/people/rewind/1999/08/07/godard
A personal assessment of Jean-Luc Godard's career trajectory, written by Charles Taylor for the always interesting Salon.com.

http://www.sensesofcinema.com
This highbrow online journal has authoritative analyses of most of the major New Wave directors and some individual film reviews. Caroline E Layde's piece on Jacques Demy is particularly interesting.

POCKET ESSENTIALS **FILM** STOCK TITLES

1903047005	Alfred Hitchcock NE Paul Duncan 4.99
1903047463	Animation Mark Whitehead 4.99
1903047676	Audrey Hepburn Ellen Cheshire 3.99
1903047587	Blaxploitation Films Mikel J Koven 3.99
1903047129	Brian de Palma John Ashbrook 3.99
1903047579	Bruce Lee Simon B Kenny 3.99
190404803X	Carry On Films Mark Campbell 4.99
1903047811	Clint Eastwood Michael Carlson 3.99
190304703X	Coen Brothers Cheshire/Ashbrook 4.99
1903047196	Doctor Who Mark Campbell 4.99
1903047633	Film Music Paul Tonks 3.99
1903047080	Film Noir Paul Duncan 3.99
1904048080	Film Studies Andrew M Butler 4.99
190304748X	Filming on a Microbudget NE Paul Hardy 4.99
1903047943	George Lucas James Clarke 3.99
1904048013	German Expressionist Films Paul Cooke 3.99
1904048145	Hal Hartley Jason Wood 3.99
1904048110	Hammer Films John McCarty 3.99
1903047382	Horror Films Le Blanc/Odell 3.99
1903047102	Jackie Chan Le Blanc/Odell 3.99
1903047951	James Cameron Brian J Robb 3.99
1903047242	Jane Campion Ellen Cheshire 3.99
1903047374	John Carpenter Le Blanc/Odell 3.99
1903047250	Krzystzof Kieslowski Monika Maurer 3.99
1903047668	Martin Scorsese Paul Duncan 4.99
1903047595	The Marx Brothers Mark Bego 3.99
1903047846	Michael Mann Mark Steensland 3.99
1903047641	Mike Hodges Mark Adams 3.99
1903047927	Oliver Stone Michael Carlson 3.99
1903047048	Orson Welles Martin Fitzgerald 3.99
1904084366	Quentin Tarantino D.K. Holm £4.99
1903047560	Ridley Scott Brian Robb 4.99
1904048102	Roger Corman Mark Whitehead 3.99
1903047897	Roman Polanski Daniel Bird 3.99
1903047277	Slasher Movies Mark Whitehead 3.99
1904048072	Spike Lee Darren Arnold 3.99
1903047013	Stanley Kubrick Paul Duncan 3.99
190304782X	Steven Soderbergh Jason Wood 3.99
1903047145	Terry Gilliam John Ashbrook 3.99
1903047625	Tim Burton Le Blanc/Odell 4.99
190304717X	Vampire Films Le Blanc/Odell 3.99
1903047935	Vietnam War Movies Jamie Russell 3.99
1903047056	Woody Allen Martin Fitzgerald 3.99
1903047471	Writing a Screenplay John Costello 4.99

Available from all good bookshops or send a cheque to: **Pocket Essentials** (Dept SS), P.O. Box 394, Harpenden, Herts, AL5 1XJ. Please make cheques payable to **'Oldcastle Books'**, add 50p for postage and packing for each book in the UK and £1 elsewhere.

US customers can send $8.95 plus $1.95 postage and packing for each book payable to; **Trafalgar Square Publishing**, PO Box 257, Howe Hill, North Pomfret, Vermont 05053, USA email tsquare@sover.net

Customers worldwide can order online at www.pocketessentials.com